Words for a Deaf Daughter

is a song of life in the midst of calamity, a precious account of how meaning can be carved into the randomness that seems to pervade our lives. There are descriptive passages in the book that burn themselves into the mind . . . an account of Mandy's vocabulary that is a stunning feat of writing. The book is addressed to Mandy, but its words go far beyond her and reach all who reckon themselves human."

—*The New York Times Book Review*

"The book is written in faith, in hope, and in love, to a dearly beloved child. Mandy is a most fortunate girl, for few other parents could possibly do as her father—sample her world."

—*The Minneapolis Tribune*

Other SIGNET Books You Will Want to Read

☐ **P.S. YOUR NOT LISTENING by Eleanor Craig.** You will never forget this wonderful teacher's story of her work with five emotionally disturbed children and her battle to make them face the real world and survive. "Has an appeal as deep as it is wide."—**Publishers Weekly**
(#J7329—$1.95)

☐ **I NEVER PROMISED YOU A ROSE GARDEN by Joanne Greenberg.** A beautifully written novel of rare insight about a young girl's courageous fight to regain her sanity in a mental hospital.
(#W7430—$1.50)

☐ **THE STORY OF SANDY by Susan Stanhope Wexler.** The moving true story of a foster parent's courageous fight for the sanity of a deeply disturbed little boy. (#Y6437—$1.25)

☐ **THE AUTOBIOGRAPHY OF A SCHIZOPHRENIC GIRL by Marguerite Sechehaye.** The classic case history of a young girl who retreats completely into a world of fantasy, and her slow recovery.
(#Q5481—95¢)

☐ **ONE FLEW OVER THE CUCKOO'S NEST by Ken Kesey.** A powerful, brilliant novel about a boisterous rebel who swaggers into the ward of a mental institution and takes over. (#E7418—$1.75)

☐ **LISA BRIGHT AND DARK by John Neufeld.** Lisa is slowly going mad but her symptoms, even an attempted suicide, fail to alert her parents or teachers to her illness. She finds compassion only from her three girlfriends who band together to provide what they call "group therapy."
(#Y6627—$1.25)

THE NEW AMERICAN LIBRARY, INC.,
P.O. Box 999, Bergenfield, New Jersey 07621

Please send me the SIGNET BOOKS I have checked above. I am enclosing $_____(check or money order—no currency or C.O.D.'s). Please include the list price plus 35¢ a copy to cover handling and mailing costs. (Prices and numbers are subject to change without notice.)

Name_____

Address_____

City_____State_____Zip Code_____

Allow at least 4 weeks for delivery

Words for a Deaf Daughter

by Paul West

A SIGNET BOOK
NEW AMERICAN LIBRARY
TIMES MIRROR

Parts 1, 2, and 7 first appeared in New American
Review Number 3, April, 1968, in rather different form.

Copyright © 1968, 1970 by Paul West.

All rights reserved. No part of this book may be used or
reproduced in any manner whatsoever without
written permission except in the case of brief quotations
embodied in critical articles and reviews.
For information address Harper & Row, Publishers, Inc.,
10 East 53 Street, New York, New York 10022.

Library of Congress Catalog Card Number: 75-95989

This is an authorized reprint of a hardcover edition
published by Harper & Row. The hardcover edition was
published simultaneously in Canada by
Fitzhenry & Whiteside Limited, Toronto.

 SIGNET TRADEMARK REG. U.S. PAT. OFF. AND FOREIGN COUNTRIES
REGISTERED TRADEMARK—MARCA REGISTRADA
HECHO EN CHICAGO, U.S.A.

SIGNET, SIGNET CLASSICS, MENTOR, PLUME AND MERIDIAN BOOKS
are published by The New American Library, Inc.,
1301 Avenue of the Americas, New York, New York 10019

FIRST PRINTING, JANUARY, 1973

5 6 7 8 9 10 11 12

PRINTED IN THE UNITED STATES OF AMERICA

Contents

1. Walk Don't Run — 7
2. All the Grades of Sandpaper — 32
3. Birds — 58
4. Babel 100 Plus — 80
5. Arabian Prelude to a Night — 112
6. Refund from Alpha 3 — 141
7. The Pink Forest Canal Society — 164

1.

Walk Don't Run

Coming into this room for the first time, they all flinch and stare at what hangs from the eight-foot cord stretched between the bay window and the inside one of frosted glass that flanks the hallway, admitting light but throwing faces into distorted silhouette.

The second and third times they still flinch and stare, but not as frightened. And even we, coming in from the dusk when it is too dark to see the leaves on the low branches your toes flick when you ride high on your swing, wince at the gallery of hanged midgets swaying in non-unison as our arrival disturbs the air around them. Hush. Whisper who dares: Christopher Robin *refuses* to say his prayers.

From left to right this is the present complement (although not the constant one, for any day you might substitute a paratrooper, a dog, or an ordinary doll):

one golliwog, crayoned in black on white paper, attached with Scotch tape having holly and berries on it—a round, vacant smile fixed since last Christmas;

a silver girl who is you bathing in a canary-yellow bath with red taps;

a hugged-shabby golliwog, three-dimensional and not scissored out of cardboard—back of head toward us and maybe no face remaining;

then, big as you, Nosferatu, adapted from an early Dracula movie but modified to fit your own unspoken but explicit preferences and so meriting a sentence to himself. His face is a yellow canvas Halloween mask with thin black mandarin mustache smeared on in charcoal; one eyehole spills lipstick blood down the side of his nose and the other is plugged with a cognac cork; the forehead wrinkles are weals lined with—what was it?—mascara or eyebrow pencil; the rest of him, corrugated cardboard pieces which once enveloped books on Galápagos birds and a whole miniature farm, we painted either with ink (his royal-blue coat) or in mauve and green stripes of poster color (the drainpipe trousers encasing those rickety legs that don't exist), letting him dry out before affixing five crimson buttons, four square floral coasters for pockets, an outsize pacifier against his right kneecap, a six-coil winding of string about his left leg, a hearing aid in each ear (like you) made of spare wire and a plastic bottle cap, and —at the extremities of each limb—white paper claws, curling and tipped red with nail varnish. He broods and leers, the major presence on the line; and no wonder, actually, for I think you force-dried him at the fire while I was out of the house hunting supplies.

That makes *two* sentences, I know. Saying it makes three.

And he is smoking a real, stubbed-out cigarette in a rolled-paper holder resembling a spent firework.

Four sentences, you see. Five. Never mind: someone who is no respecter of appearances has stuck a face of arsenical green against his right shoulder, so he looks both beheaded and not, the one head not quite underneath his arm (but tilting that way, so he *could* if he wished walk the Bloody Tower like him in the song), the other head erect in a sentinel's aloofness, banana-yellow-bald. If we sit beneath him on the sofa that isn't near enough the wall to catch windfalls from the line, which happen when the Scotch tape has dried out, the claws on his right foot float against the backs of our heads. When you yourself sit, they float above you like hooks ready to hoist you up to join the figures in the air. But you never go, in spite of your passion for standing on window sills, riding escalators to the top of every building, sitting voluptuously at the tops of slides. You are content to have them over you, watching, presiding, eavesdropping perhaps; guardian angels, furies, and gargoyles all in one; paper-edge sharp, paper-frail, paint- or crayon-static; household gods always in need of repair and whom, from time to time, you console for their thinness by adding a real golly or two to the line.

Interrupting myself, if I may, I know that in school at this very moment you'll be matching and naming colors in the room whose door bears the imperative, in the ITA spelling, WAUK. And some of them tell you not to run, the doors I mean. I'm certainly moving through your household gods at *wauk*ing speed but, then, you and I do our fair share of running when you come home, and I, doing my best to contort my face into a likeness of Nosferatu's, have to chase you up the stairs or round the apple trees, both eaters and cookers.

Back now to where *I* was. Next there's a crew-cut golliwog painted in garish quarters, then a multi-spotted clown superimposed over a golliwog in baggy breeches (like the Dutch boys in your books who stuck their fingers in the dike to keep the sea back). For eight inches, now, the line holds nothing save a transparent slip of Scotch tape like 8mm film hung blankly out to dry; on this, once, hung the clown who now, hooked into a string loop by his egregious head horn, blots out the Dutch golliwog. There follow five more creations: an eager, alert golliwog in red-striped shirt but minus feet; a pike-nosed Japanese fighter plane called the Kawasaki Hien, camouflaged green and gray and cut out from the lid of the box the kit came in, the decals like blood moons; another golliwog, also Dutch, with an oafish grin and, stuck on his left leg like a cannibal trophy, a mustached man in military uniform; a lime-green clown whose legs come trunking out from the base of his neck, and whose face is a skull; and an armless purple gorilla in vermilion jeans. At the line's end hangs your own contribution, a red triangle trimmed with white fluff—a Santa Claus's hat on which you stuck a miniature of Santa himself, whom you call "Beard." A quick look down and we find your print, in a frame, of "Boy with Dove" (Picasso, born 1881, eighty years before you), the boy's face emptied of emotion as he looks into the middle or the far distance with the dove at his chin. Last, the budgerigar in his cage and the sliding glass partition you once butted with your corn-haired head and smashed.

Why tell you what you know? Maybe the reasons are selfish; but when, if ever, you read this, you will have forgotten your years of infant *Sturm und Drang* as well as the comparative idyll of this, your second year in school. A year ago, after you had been at school only a month, they divided you up for the annual report issued in the month of birth (and found you baffling). Here it is, including the by now almost classical reference to your right convergent squint, especially when looking into cameras. Your lip-reading rubric has this beneath it: *Understands familiar words through lip-reading and hearing. Span of attention for assimilating new vocabulary is still short.* Yes, and I know you can be incorrigibly frivolous about new words, few of which you ever seem to think you need; but I have also seen you checking through your physiognomy at a mirror, saying the words loudly and almost correctly while the bits of head they denote remain in place. As they say in the report under Speech Aptitude, you imitate *many sounds very well, with an accurate reproduction of intonation too;* but they go on to note how you are *easily distracted from concentrated speech work* (so was I, if it's any comfort to you, until about twenty-five). Always, you have taken or left speech, as you thought fit; and no bribe or coercion will work, but only a counter-distraction equivalent to gold over silver, radioactivity over magnetism, Samarkand over Acapulco, or—if things are really bad—*sambur,* the Indian elk, over such familiars as a plastic mouse and a double-jointed toy poodle, hose pipe over water pistol, a foot-long pencil made of rock candy (disguised as an umbrella) over anything that writes. The house is crammed with gaudy attention getters we used to use, both at home and at the audiology clinic, just to get you to *look*—and as soon as you looked we, they, took the baubles away in order to work with what attention you gave while it lasted. Which often wasn't long: time for a word, a plosive, a round O, concessions you perfunctorily made to the word-obsessed rest of the world.

Next among your school souvenirs-to-come (their souvenirs of you) I find something beguilingly titled Kindergarten Occupations ("including Pre-Reading and Elementary Numbers," which according to a Harvard seminar that includes a few brilliant children is arbitrary anyway). Here again you have a good beginning, as I well know, having seen you mount an insensate fury because I had drawn a figure with only one leg, or, more refinedly provoking, only one eyebrow: *Discrimination,* I read, *between shapes, colors, and sizes is accurate and she draws meaning from simple pictures but not yet from the written word, nor yet from numbers, spoken or written.* As for your Manual Skills— you who paint astounding abstracts, which you sometimes populate with people who are globeheads on single stems—you come out well: *Controls scissors, pencils, and brushes well and manipulates small parts of con-*

structional toys. Paintings show an interest in color and her drawings a liking for pattern. They may not know it, they may not remember it (but I think they *were* told): your interest in color used to extend to painting your whole face green with eye shadow, thus converting yourself into something between a chlorophyll goblin and a fugitive from a horror film. Also, you painted windows, daubed walls, both inside and out, and laughingly improvised pigments from anything at hand —instant coffee plus plaster of Paris plus Ajax cleanser plus ink, all for windows and walls and carpets, the top of my desk, the mail and papers as they arrived. And soot! Let's be kind to each other and forget about soot. Of pattern, all I'll say is that your passion for design and symmetry would have done credit to a medieval theologian. Somewhere in your head you kept a kind of DNA pattern of the attitudes and millimetrical relationships in which you wanted things to be—slippers, cutlery, cushions, curtains, rugs, and pokers, all such. I have seen you rage because, somewhere in the house, there was a bottle with an imperfectly replaced top, or because someone was engorging with the wrong spoon. If there is to be an argument from design, then at some point you must surely have been dispatched to earth as a special proof.

Let's look at Physical Education. They say—in what strikes me as consummate understatement—that you are *energetic,* which is like calling the cheetah not backward in moving forward or the elephant heavier than air. Or, say, a laser beam equal to the chore of wax melting. A compulsive, rapid, and exquisitely coordinated mover, you have overrun us all while working out of your system something that you inhale back again with each breath; and so, on it goes, this unquenchable agitation of your legs and arms that never quite matches the rhythm of your high-pitched, looping call. You never lose balance, trip, skid, misjudge a distance, or cannon into things you don't in any case intend to wreck. Throwing, though, you use both your arms and legs and then throw backward with a lovely inconsequentiality it is hard to mimic (though we try, wanting to know how it feels). In this case, movement is all, and destination is as much beside the point as the parabola the thrown thing makes. School found you enjoyed P.E., but also that you tend to keep to familiar apparatus; then they added, *Does not comprehend Musical Movement, but joins in when encouraged.* But you rock, when consoling yourself, in a perfect rhythm, just like the Olympic flip-jumper Dick Fosbury when he is preparing to take off. It's only when you try to dance that you settle for dynamic cavort in lieu of the specific timing and pattern that most mortals—for reasons which I confess have always eluded me—try to move to. You—well, let's say you are closer to Nijinsky or Zorba the Greek than to Fred Astaire.

The report's concluding long entry comments on your Social Development, an aspect of your life which— because people would never let their children play with you for reasons you never knew about—only began with school. Up to then, you played with adults and aped adult ways. *Plays happily,* the report says, *alongside other children but does not enter into their play, nor join in easily with group activities, although her interest in what the other children are doing is increasing.* Simply, you had never had any practice, had not realized that suddenly you were permitted to play with other children. I have never seen you refuse to play with any consenting adult in private or in public; but, of course, then you played exceeding rough, and only the hardiest among the adults consented a second time. Torn hair, bashed nose, rent lapels, fingernailed eyes, and brutalized privates, these were the stigmata you bestowed. I remember the playing and the mythologies it suggested: a commando course supervised by an overwhelming midget; *Götterdämmerung* written in mud, rain, and your own bland wee; Herculean tests in the presence of a three-foot warbling Zeus whose fists pounded us further and further into muscle-snapping contortions until we felt we had lived in the Augean stables since the year One, the venue always liberally swilled by yourself with floods of water or littered with hillocks of refuse. Given knowledge, strength, and time, you would certainly have converted any aircraft hangar into a play area approximating—by what your own ideals were then—a diluvial hell, a bulge with alligators which paradoxically sang like linnets, adults who melted at the first hit of your spit (and then weirdly remanifested themselves as gigantic umbrellas with big rancid lettuce leaves for fabric); eagles and buzzards (whose appearance you seemed to fancy in your picture books) and herring gulls (which you bared your teeth at and, maybe, expected one day to fight on even terms, having taken off while running like the wind beneath them). Those things certainly would be part of any master plan of yours, but also—if I'm getting it right—coal, sand, polyunsaturated oil, and broken glass, hammers and shovels and knives, mayonnaise to slick your eel body with and soft nougat to plaster down your spilling hair.

The last comment on you reads, with bleak simplicity: *Difficult to assess. (Brain damage?)* The question mark sums up a great deal of the considerable amount said about you over the past years and either canceled out or left dubiously standing. It is clear that, more often than occasionally, something in your head doesn't work as it ought to; something that seems tied up with your hearing's poorness. What? I wish I knew. The words that crop up—brain damage, middle-brain damage, nerve deafness, autism, dyslexia, etc.—give us no more than an illusion of command, or of knowing, yet I know of parents who, wanting passionately to have their child diagnosed, refuse the specific label when it comes. In the semi-dark of not knowing, we go ahead and treat you as only deaf and encourage you to progress at a speed that doesn't compound your difficulties. Whatever might be the total or the explanation of the things wrong with you, let me tell you—in case, maybe, you've been too busy to realize it—exuberant play and emphatic response have worked minor wonders with you already; so has school, and so has (I presume) the battery of tiny rituals you've evolved in play. *Ee-ya,* you say when things are going well, a gentle rocking sound which, made under the roof of your mouth, announces you are happy and intend to prolong that condition by repeating its vocal signal.

And *ee-ya* we ourselves have got into the habit of saying, even when you're not around. I wouldn't waste such a *trouvaille* for worlds; but, then, I couldn't really write you a whole letter of *ee-ya,* even when that sound expresses the mood I usually feel. Hence, all these words, a surprise package for you and your introduction to people who'd want to know you. You wake each day, uncertain if the world is still there: you check the garden to see if your slide has survived the darkness or merely several hours of your not having used it; you do much the same when you come home from school. In fact, without our knowing it, you probably check a dozen treasures in a whole burst of intermittent apprehension; so thank goodness things don't move of their own accord, slides dissolve in rain, swings work themselves up overnight and lunge off above the trees in elated orbit. Your love of pattern comes from—it's obvious, isn't it?—your deep sense of precariousness in a world of near silence. You're both the tyrant and the victim of categories, locations, and Mercator fixes. Not only do you want everything in its place; you even devise new places for things whose places didn't seem sure enough: the gray velvet elephant kneeling in the window you have thrust forward upon his trunk, and there in that position he must stay; he used to stand straight elsewhere, but *where* you have brainwashed us into forgetting. So too with the alarm clocks, which you have appropriated to your bedside table, asserting a multiple claim not so much on time itself (of which you are almost heedless) as on rattling bells held repeatedly against your right ear, the one through which a little contraband-like sound comes in. Somehow, if things are where you think they ought to be, they do better than otherwise what they are supposed to do.

And yet, and yet (I would be more confident deciphering some ancient stone whose writings use an unknown alphabet), once you have set in order and in place all you think that matters, you shower it with your own special confetti of toffee wrappers, popsicle sticks, ripped newspapers, string, rubber bands, hair clips, and crayon shavings, as well as small items of potato salad, breakfast cereal, and unfinished vanilla ices. It's as if, having designed and erected Stonehenge or seen the ground plan of Leptis Magna, you can happily ignore weeds that thrive or sand that amasses. You don't, as they say, pick up after you; but, with your geometer's knowledge of where things are under or among the clutter (assuming no creep has interfered with them), you race over and round and among them with batlike accuracy, only occasionally reversing to bestow a heel tap of delicate acknowledgment—for being there to be circumvented at all, but, having been circumvented, having to be gone back to out of a kind of Rube Goldberg civility mixed with collector's pride. (You'd have understood Samuel Johnson's *having* to touch all the hitching posts as he went down Fleet Street.) Courier, acrobat and pirouetting elf in one, you pay daily homage to the just-so-ness man can achieve. You have little idea, yet, of surname, and none of address, city and country, but you know where the *wun, tω, three* counting chart belongs, which coat goes on which hook, which hair clip is missing from which side of your head. *Oi-ya!* you howl when things have been displaced, a cry that climbs until it seems to rend our skulls and then dives in curt exasperation. *Ee-ya,* you coo when things have been set where they belong, when the matching hair clip has been reinstalled; and there you are in a contained ecstasy that finds all planets behaving well around your sun and passes meteors by without a glance.

An "exceptional" child (to use a term whose very precision wins a bonus from the word's conventional link with cleverness), you astound me as jugglers and mystics and astronauts do. You didn't seem unusual—not to mention exceptional—until you were two. Up to then you fooled everyone, including the doctor and your observant big sister; your excellent lip-reading carried you that far, and I salute the tremendous and spontaneous effort you made in thus responding to the only normality you knew. A tiny girl, you self-helped yourself to somewhere just below average until the colossal odds against you showed you up. Slow to speak, you were cautious about starting to walk; but once you had walked you ran like a bird preparing to take off. You fell in love, as well, with water and umbrellas, and in the presence of either orated vehemently (although non-verbally) to yourself. Water you preferred in puddles on the living-room floor or in baths, but you also liked it in rainspouts, saucepans, and lavatory basins. Umbrellas—which, I think, exerted the stronger spell—you collected with casual relentlessness. You never had fewer than a dozen. They were your trees, really: a plastic-leaved, tin-branched orchard of them, which every night had to be rolled up firm and laid across your bed, and every morning landed in a cascade on ours when you came heavy-footedly in, hooting for them to be opened. Then, with half-blind eyes, down to the living room where we spread them over the floor like Pan and Company afforesting a bare mountain while you, red-cheeked with elation, danced among them, catching occasionally the beads on the rib ends and skimming the canopies half round, but never trampling the handles or ramming a fist through the fabric.

You would stand, do a preliminary skip to get your timing right—a one-two-three with your big toes creased downward as if to scratch earth—and then flow into a joyous high-kneed pounding, your long hair a flash, your arms providing you with a tightrope walker's balance, your eyes unobtainably fixed on an upper corner of the room, where you saw what no one else saw. You looked and smiled, and danced the more wildly for it, fueling your semi-tarantella from the presence in the vacancy. *Fred,* we began to say, domesticating the ghost; *it's Fred again.* And so, each morning, with a flim and a flam, and a flim again, followed by a swift series of flim-flams, you danced spread-eagled, lithe and bony, chirping on an empty stomach.

It was winter when we flew you to the university clinic in a Viscount which lurched through the rain above the heaving, pumice-gray sea. At each plunge or sideslip you let out a birdcall of delight. Born on the island, home of witches, banshees, and temperamental goblins, you had never been off it. And now, leaving it for the first time, you seemed isolated in a new way. Your three words—*baba, more* and *ish-ish*—you had used heroically, intending meanings we missed and being credited with others that we invented. I listened to the lax, feathered whine of the engines, wondering what noise they made to you as you sat smiling into the clouds through the tall oval of the window. I'd heard, I told myself, on humid days the squeak of my sinuses filling, and then a pop of contraction on a day of high pressure, with all the sinews and membranes tugging and fluctuating in a mucous orchestration. But that was nothing to what I imagined for your own head: a tinnitus of bad bells, a frying noise, which in combination drove you to cup a hand over your right ear and rock heavily to that side as if trying to shake something loose or back into place or—thought ended: the two-foot doll, bathed with you every night in the bathroom and brought with you on the plane, slipped sideways from your casual hug, and a cache of bath water spilled into your lap. *My* fault, I said: you can't blame a stark-naked doll.

When we landed, you whooped down the steps from the plane. It was still raining, but we had two umbrellas, both yours. The only trouble was that you didn't want them open or up; they had to be carried before us like totems, one red, the other green, every loose fold clamped tight by a rubber band. Two umbrellas kept from being wet made good folk stare; but good folk knew nothing of umbrellas, water, and you. In the taxi, however, you opened up the red umbrella and sat in an indifferent silence, an erect-sitting being of utter trustfulness, heedless of the roof lining you might puncture, and with no more idea of where you were going than of where you had come from. Out of the taxi, you insisted, with a plangent squeak, on the umbrella's being folded again and rebound in its rubber band. Then you were ready to march with us past the porter's lodge (empty), wrongly up steps to the Department of Law and down again, and finally into a waiting room stocked with heavy ridable toys, and equipped with tiny toilets whose still water you inspected and approved.

Called for, we went left into the laboratory (one wall of which was a one-way window facing a lecture room). You stared at the people, the things, and, it seemed, at Fred, whom you have always been able to find anywhere. You grew busy and began to chirp. When, to your exact satisfaction, you had arranged the umbrellas and the doll on a low table, you turned to the experts with a patronizing smile. We sat and watched—your mother at one end of the room, myself (still feeling damp) at the other—helpless on the perimeter and unable to smoke. There was some tinkering with a green box, all dials, and a chart. The door snicked open, admitting an authoritative face which beamed and vanished. Then testing began with overtures of friendship from the studious-mannered man whose trousers looked as if he kneeled a lot. The calm woman in patent-leather high heels clicked a tiny clicker, but you did not turn. They gave you a doll then and tried you from behind with a duck quack, a whistle of low pitch, several rattles, then a small tom-tom. Abruptly, not having turned, you ran to the table, slammed one doll alongside the other and hooted, with finger pointed, for the red umbrella to be opened. There were nods; the umbrella opened, sprang taut, was set in your hands, and you squatted, drawing it down over your head as if sheltering under a thin, frail mushroom, slipping out a hand to adjust a downslid sock, and beginning to make again the birdcall (as if a curlew tried to bleat) which had driven countless local dogs into emulative frenzy, provoked birds into surpassing themselves (searching for a bird, they never saw *you*), and scared all the cats away.

Private under the panels of vinyl, you sang with mounting fervor, the umbrella stem between your legs. No one moved. It was clear that you were going to be given your leisure, allowed to collect yourself. In succession you fluted your voice upward in an ecstatic trill, twirled the umbrella like a color disc without once catching the rim or the plastic against your face (a perfect, sheltering fit it was), peeped out to giggle just a bit fearfully, hoisted the umbrella up and away behind you in a pose from *The Mikado*, and then hid again beneath it. We had seen your face shining with heat, seen you only long enough for that.

Now they tapped on your roof, flicked middle finger hard off thumb against the fabric, and brought their mouths close to the surface, calling your name. Out you came, astounded at something heard: not your name, because you didn't know it then, but something—a retaliating and envious dog, a curlew weary of being competed with, a cat returning to venture a duet—amplified and vibrating in the umbrella above you, but only faces and maneuvering mouths to make it. Us. Us only; so you concealed yourself again, tilting the canopy forward.

What brought you out again and kept you out was the xylophone. You abandoned the umbrella for it, fondled it a while, then beat the living decibels out of it, a Lionel Hampton Lilliputian who struck away and then canted your ear close to the trembling bars, your eyes widening in half-piqued recognition that *this* was what we'd flown you across the sea for. You banged on it with the wooden hammer a few times more and let it fall the two and a half feet to the parquet, wincing once in the wrong direction as it hit.

After calls, hums, hisses, pops, buzzes, barks, bays, and several indeterminate ululations, all from behind you, they did the left side while you smiled at a distracting monkey puppet over on the right. My hands were holding each other too tightly; your mother, twelve yards down the room, looked pale, her maternity shut painfully off and her own hands beginning gestures that ended halfway, the fingers tongue-tied.

"Now," said the studious kneeling man, his kindly face tense, and snapped two wooden bars together. A slapstick, I thought, like the split lath of the harlequin. But whatever was going on, it wasn't low comedy. What he said next, after a fractional shake of his head to the woman in heels—the professional pair's exchange of glances crossing the parental one—sounded like:

"Right down the track." The headshake was a zero in mime.

You smiled at the puppet, offering your hand to put inside it. They let you, working through all the modes of sound, but not to a crescendo, only to a punctuational drum tap, which you ignored. And then, as the light waned—that legendary dank Manchester light swollen with soot and rain and absorbed by tons on tons of Victorian brick and tile—they switched sides, this time beguiling you with a model farm at which you sat, cantankerously checking the cows for udders (as a country girl should) and stationing Clydesdale horses at the water trough. Brilliants of wet formed along your nose and you heard not the snap-crack of the wooden bars; not the first time, anyway. But when it came from a yard closer—these testers gliding about the room like prankish Druids—you flinched, directed an offended stare in a vaguely right-hand direction, and went back to your farm. Again and again they worked from the right, varying the angle and the sound. Again and again, with just a few moments of preoccupied indifference, you jerked your head sideways, beginning to be cheerful as you discovered the routine: beginning to play.

Suddenly there was no farm. It went into a gray steel cabinet against which you kicked and at which you took a running kick as your eyes began to pour (tears whopping enough, I thought, to merit nostrils for conduits) and your birdcall harshened. As you swung, both-handed, the xylophone at the locked handle of the door, I got up, stuck out a hand as I half-fell in a skid on the polish, and took a tonic sol-fa smack in the forehead as you swung the instrument backward again, farther than before, the better to mangle the steel between you and the authentic cows, the horses a-thirsting.

"Ap," I sort of said through the plong and the blank

crash, not seeing well. "You might as well get it out again."

"Naughty girl," your mother said unconvincedly as you laugh-cried, pitching the xylophone over your shoulder without so much as a look. I have seen you dispose in the same way of bus tickets, mail, money, books, food, scissors, and plates. The oubliette is anywhere behind you.

"She'll soon—" I heard, but the rest was drowned by a scream of unmitigated anger while you pounded the cabinet with both fists.

"Strong!" called the man who kneeled a lot, busying himself with earphones attached to the many-dialed machine. "She's a grand temper."

"You've seen nothing," I told him. "Yet." I knew how, in the Cleopatra-Clytemnestra rages to which you entitled and still entitle yourself, you could butt your head through a firm window (one so far, without bloodshed, but there were long blond hairs on the splinters of glass). Or pound your uncallused hand down through the crisp and warm pulp of a loaf not long out of the oven, once burying your hand and bringing your arm up with a bread mallet wedged on your wrist, crying, "Ish! Ish!" which is anthem, plea, and threat in one.

But it wasn't *Ish* you came out with this time; it was the first of your calls, *Baba—babababa,* uttered with pauses only long enough for everyone present to shout the same phonemes back at you. If we didn't, you increased the volume, blustering and raucous. It was the most comprehensive aural version of yourself. So the clinic room, soundproof of course (there is even a sign just inside the entrance requesting silence), became a barnyard for a while. Turning wet-eyed, grime-faced, to each of us in turn, you babbled at us, coercing, commanding, appealing; and in turn and sometimes in unison we babbled and brayed back, short only of a cock-a-doodle-doo, the hymn of a pig wallowing or even farrowing in hot lava, and a moose drowning in a swamp of caviar. This, so that the testing could go on: one farmyard for another.

In the beginning is the test, and in the end comes a remedy of sorts. But how, I wondered, can they even begin—overworked but obliged not to rush; never short of children to work with, one in six hundred being somehow deaf and usually not deaf only—until they too have run their fingers across the crowns of the blunt, curiously thick, small teeth you had then, have seen you dance a full hour among the umbrellas, have night after night studied your fanatical attention to the placing of your slippers within an invisible outline which is there and symmetrical for you beneath the chest of drawers in your bedroom. . . . As you were then: now you have new teeth, you dance less among umbrellas and fuss less about slippers; but how I felt hasn't gone at all.

"You haven't—" I began to say on our third trip to the clinic, seen her do the living things: give Creation a run for its money. Not at home. They hadn't seen you, like a gross Ophelia, distribute around the house —on the window ledges, in the wardrobe between two decent suits or dresses, on the rim of the letter box, on the Christmas tree itself—pork sausages on butcher's hooks or threaded on wire coat hangers. Or eat the sausage raw, oblivious of worms. Or, in hydrodynamic delight, rip off shoes and socks to plant your bare feet on the TV screen whenever it showed water. Or (I stopped: they were calling your name again and you weren't ever going to answer) sit naked and warbling for an hour in a washbasin of cold water. Or green your face, eat nail varnish, coat the windows with lavender furniture polish, jump down five stairs fearlessly, mimic (by waving a stiffened arm) men carrying umbrellas, chant into a toilet pedestal after choking it with a whole roll of tissue, chew cigarettes, cover yourself with Band-aids when there wasn't a scratch in sight, climb any ladder and refuse to descend, slide pencils up your nose, use a rubber hammer on the doctor's private parts, drink from your potty, wade into a sewer-inspection chamber the plumber had opened, eat six bananas in six minutes, wind and play those alarm clocks at your right ear again and again, shave your face and arms and legs with instant lather and bladeless razor, threaten enormous dogs by advancing upon them with a reed in hand, cut your own hair at random, dissolve soap in a tin basin, rock so hard that your hair touched the floor on either side, sit motionless and rapt in front of a mirror, voluminously autograph walls, tear samples from the dictionary or a book of Picasso prints, stare unblinking into 150-watt bulbs, run, run, run everywhere, heedless of gesticulating and half-felled adults and the sanity of drivers. Exclusive, you even collected and threw away all the keys in the house. . . .

"Mandy . . . *Mandy* . . . MANDY," said the folk at the clinic, upping the volume as you gazed from them to the red finger spinning across the dial and back again. When you heard them, your expression changed, fixing in atavistic wonder. It was as if we were watching the face of sound itself while you, flushed and nervous, heard something visible. After an interval they let you use the microphone yourself, and you began to boom and call in an almost continuous orgy of sound, confronted for the first time with your own share of the missing continent: a Columbus of euphony dumbfoundedly exclaiming at the glories of exclamation itself, every bit like the man in Xenophon who kept shouting *thalassa!* when he saw the sea. I myself felt a bit like shouting; I'd never heard anyone hearing before. And since then I've known a good many firsts with you— things which, up to then, I'd done without really experiencing them, or which you yourself thought up and

I myself had never dreamed of doing. Some of the latter are grotesque and sometimes rather revolting as well; I try not to do them, but usually you prevail, imperious queen with your dithering court. I do as I am told. Most people would, just as unquestioningly as Louis XIV's courtiers at Versailles asked for admission by scraping on the door with the elongated nail of the little finger otherwise used for ear cleaning.

It's four years since that first visit to the clinic when powerlessness hit home to us. The strain told on you too. You fetched a shovel from the garden to destroy with: lighting fixtures, windows, crockery, clocks. Strong always, you lifted and swung it with ease, pouting with birdcall. It took you two years to reject the shovel, to change from indefatigable and destructive hobgoblin into a girl who, gaining a word a month only to lose it the month after, developed big, Nordic, luminously beautiful features. Capable, without warning, of histrionic graciousness of manner (as if all the pressures lifted at once and the noises in your head stopped) you enjoyed your increasingly frequent visits to the clinic (toys, earphones, EEG apparatus), ate mightily, hardly ever caught a cold, thumped obliviously past staring or derisive children, and rebaffled the experts. Deaf, yes; "stone" deaf (in that melodramatic inversion of the pathetic fallacy) in the left ear; autistic, perhaps, but that's a vague word like "romantic"; brain damage not ruled out; amblyopia mentioned, with an ophthalmologist joining your team.

At five, blasé by now about Viscounts, you went to live near the clinic and the school associated with it (*one* of the schools, I should say). I signed out a speech trainer, on which you had a daily lesson, dealing sometimes in words, sometimes in sheer noise. You did your jigsaws like an impatient robot, began to lip-read, and gradually built up and kept a tiny vocabulary enunciated with almost coy preciosity, intoning "more" like an aria, raising "hair" into "har," curtailing "mouth" into "mou," lengthening "nose" into a three-second sound, but all the same *talking* although you still didn't know your name. Nicknames accumulated, but not in your presence: Moo, from Mandy-Moo; Birdie, from your call; Tish, from *ish-ish;* Lulu, developed cunningly from the two-syllable, high-pitched call with which your mother called you in and still does; Yee, which sound you yourself substituted for Baba; Proof, from the condition called Manda-proof, you being the only thing or person invulnerable to yourself, or so we said; and, strangest of all to strangers, Boat, your own word for water—until you got *worbar*—shouted while paddling your feet on the TV screen.

Epic formulae, these, while you went incognito; but, since then, other nicknames—names which augment you, eke you out as the dictionary puts it—have come and gone, while you have been busy learning and retaining your real name. Boula came from a mellow little incantation of your own (usually *boula-boo*) rhyming with "howler." Tadpole, sounding disrespectful, was and is a term of endearment somehow expressing the larval, strangely vulnerable innocence that floods across your face at times, and Spider, sounding even worse, describes you when you are all flicking legs, impossible to hold, and certain to pinch or nip, bite or scratch. East (or *The* East) is the logical extension of your contrariness (as in East West) and, in fact, brought after it the mock title of East-Priest, you being the hierophant of contrariness (if you don't mind my saying so).

Most recently, on account of the magnificent exhilaration with which you bump around in the world of home and school, we have begun to call you Jaunty, a word not much used these days but having some connection with *gentil* or *genteel* and certainly the right one for your special fusion of "easy sprightliness" with "airy self-satisfaction" (that's what the dictionary says).

I'd almost forgotten your true middle name, Klare, which we reserve for you when the hair is pulled back off your forehead, thus exposing the most babylike feature you have: *Klare without the hair,* that's what we say when your bangs are back, but also when you're being several years less than your age. Then there's Bertie, via Birdie, for when you're being unduly tomboyish; and I mustn't forget Mandy Brella, called in from the name reserves when your umbrella obsession takes you over for a whole day, and Mrs. Manda, the indefatigable, havoc-creating automaton of housework who washes wallpaper and swills down the kitchen floor with many bucketfuls of water as if it is the stony, bloodied, slippery underfoot of a slaughterhouse.

Fun for us, of course, all that; but learning who you truly were was grim for you. During one spell (I mean phase, but spell suggests also the primitive power that seemed to hold you in thrall), you averaged only three hours' sleep a night, erupting at midnight with umbrella and jigsaws, then fetching a guitar, one mechanical top, several model baths, a dish brimming with soap dissolved, a length of rusty iron piping and a purloined fruit knife, with all of which to while away the night until you could go out. And always wet. You became frenetic, twitched more than ever, during this waiting period: all that soothed you was running water, the swing in the garden, and the ghoulish faces I pulled while pursuing you—as usual—up the stairs. You partnered everyone at the lavatory, exclaiming "Oh" in exaggerative dismay at anyone's being under the vile necessity and then seeking to examine the deposit. But, we noticed, your *Yee* (or *Ee*) was less strident, less insistent; a month later, it had become a delicate, diffident greeting to be answered just as quietly, and you became drier, banged your head less, were less captivated by the grotesque or the effluvial, gave up rending the day's newspaper, lost your passion for knives, began to draw faces and bodies that had two eyes, not one, with two legs instead of a barbed-wire entanglement of blue ballpoint. You even drew a bath—always the long throne of your joy—with a Mandy in it.

You took the intelligence test and managed well before, after forty minutes' concentration, you flung the next puzzle across the room and began a blue-ribbon tantrum. The children's hospital lost your file, and two starch-bosomed nurses lost their cool when you screamed twenty minutes solid because they took from you the model jet kept to calm little boys during EEG tests. You thought it was a present—you think anything is a present (every salesman who arrives at the door with a case of samples has brought you a case of presents).

"I'll buy it," I shouted against the screams. "It's worth it." No, that was out of the question; it was part of the equipment, it was HOSPITAL PROPERTY. You vanished into the pathology lab, and were there found admiring fetuses, tumors, and cysts in their quiet jars, a true humanist explaining to you what was what. We got you a jet at the airport, and, later, a helicopter, a new model bath, a miniature cooking set in Bavarian iron, building blocks, card games, a thousand candy cigarettes, as many lollipops and ices: a surplus for purposes of habilitation, no matter what got smashed, lost, torn, or wasted, no matter what melted or disappeared into the trapped water in the lavatory.

Out of the clutter you have come a girl who can make beds (sometimes six sheets to a bed), bake bread black, fry bacon tin-hard, iron and fold clothes with all the finesse of a weight lifter, Hoover the carpets, mow the lawn, more or less set a table, adjust the TV, fell apples from the tree by swatting it with a tennis racquet, tune your own hearing aids, on your best days butter bread and on most days recite your first name. You cried and shuffled not at all when you began at the school for the deaf, a day girl, almost six. You have become unoffendably gregarious, have learned to hold hands. You look through illustrated magazines with an almost clinical gravity. You have discovered how *no* doubles your range of concepts, and you see Fred, I realize, less and less. The Martian we sometimes call you, or Miss Rabelais (two more names!). Photogenic, long and agile, you have a vocabulary, a schoolbag and a homework book, which is all penumbra to the darkness of one small girl invading the house with a big shovel, sometimes a coal hammer, and that unfailing drooped-eyelid leer.

One special thing left a new light shining (and there have been others since). Your class of nine children, working by the loop that amplifies sound identically for you all, whichever way you all turn, was told to draw a spider's web. All drew but you, who sat abstractedly apart aloof from this planet. No one saw you move— and, being thoroughly ambidextrous at that time, you could have done it with either hand—but when your teacher reached you, you were *yee*-ing gently beside a perfectly delineated web, all done in one unbroken line, with a spider at center. Just a few smudges. It went up on the classroom wall, a prized exhibit, and is now in the big roll of all your drawings, not (where I think you meant it to go) in your crate of junk in which, I once thought, you meant to bury us all, outclassed by your energy, thwarted by your privacy, heartsick at Nature's misbehavior, and as short of new expedients as of sleep.

And now, having gone this long (and having cheated by including something I'd written about, instead of to, you, on a previous occasion), I'm going to stop; there'll be more later, after later. In the meantime, here's a peace offering, to be accepted in the same spirit as it's made in. When, from time to time, I take a rest, I'll stand you one of these—nothing much but something, *some things*, to keep you going and maybe gentle you a little. Fyodor Dostoevsky, when a student of engineering at the military school, once drew up an admirable design for a fortress; but, and here's the offering, he forgot to provide it with entrances and exits.

2.

All the Grades of Sandpaper

Back to you now, if you're still receiving me. I'd thought of starting, one, two, three, thirty, umpteen, but that's not how to balance; that's not how to count the blessings compared with the cost. It's better bookkeeping to tell you that you quicken in us the sense of life and make us grateful for what's usually taken for granted. A handicap so severe as yours (and maybe I should be using the plural for its multiple kind) drives a parent through fury, then through an empty, vengeful indignation, to two points: first, when in the absence of explanations medical and reasons cosmic, he ignores the handicap *to make it go away;* second, nearer to common sense, when he welcomes it in as your special gift and, while trying to eliminate it, learns its nature by heart as a caution to himself and studies the voracious subtlety of your compensations—as when you, unlike most of us, smell at a pencil newly sharpened, inhaling from the beechwood its own soot-sour bouquet, or trace with addicted fingers the corrugations on the flat of a halved cabbage before eating it raw with the same naturalness with which you drink vinegar, steak sauce, and mayonnaise, and sniff glue. I too, now, have tasted ink (a flavor of charred toenail), coal (a rotted iron-and-yeast pill), bark (woolly and bland, suggested vulcanized crab meat), leather (a taste here not of the meat or the fat next the hide but of the fur once outside it and of seaweed iodine).

Tasting—testing—with you, I have found new ways into the world. You discover what you discover because you have lost what you've lost; or, rather, you recover what men have lost precisely because they neglect to use something which you never even had and therefore could not "lose." I tag along on your voyages of exploration, and together we sneak into the randomness, the arbitrariness, of the universe as distinct from its patterns. Without you—although I have in my time delighted in *The Compleat Angler*'s bald and mild arcana, in insect books and fungus books, in Jean Rostand's reports on tadpoles and toads—I don't think I would be delving, as I now am, with strangely relevant irrelevance, into the behavior of slugs, mushrooms, cicadas, and flesh-eating plants. Because you brandished it at a big dog, I found out about great reed mace (*Typha latifolia*), often wrongly called the bulrush, but rightly, I reckon, thought almost human. The black six-foot stem is a long cheroot, topped by a yellow spike, and, as my *Observer's Book of Wild Flowers* says, "the closely packed pistillate flowers forming the 'mace' consist of a stalked ovary, with a slender style and a one-sided, narrow stigma, and enveloped in tufts of soft, brownish hairs." A tall woman of a flower—but you can argue that one with me when you come to it in your own time.

I keep two books, one for what *you* do, one for what I find out while waiting for our first conversation. You ate a dandelion flower some time back; one day I'll try you (the genial sense) with the leaves in oil and vinegar, that good salad. I have a lot to tell you which, thank goodness, I've been late in learning; so it's fresh. The hyena isn't quite the scavenger he's supposed to be, whereas the almost extinct American bald eagle is a scavenger out and out. And so on: it's a question, really, of finding a life style, of opening up for myself a universe into which you fit. So I try to devise for you the biggest memberships possible, now and then blundering from wishful thinking into wishful biology, but at other times enrolling you in majestic clans you'd stare at if you knew about them, just as some of the inhumanly ordinary on the earth have stared at you—and still do, themselves suffering a vicarious penalty and, with their frowns, wondering why such children as you aren't put apart....

To get back. Take the shark, created perpetually with two inexplicable handicaps: it has no swim bladder, so must keep on the move or sink; its fixed, paired fins have hardly any braking effect and no motive power, which means that it finds difficulty stopping or reversing. A shark, therefore, is compulsive and a bit helpless; no one knows why. Or take the bulbul bird, the fruit-eating bat, the guinea pig, and man, who alone among known species cannot make their own vitamin C; the reason for this inborn metabolic flaw no one knows. But *all* sharks and bulbul birds and fruit-eating bats and guinea pigs and men are handicapped in these respective ways, whereas what I'm casting around for is a handicap not just inexplicable but also affecting just a few specimens only.

Trying again, I come up with the Mexican amphibian, the axolotl, which instead of becoming a salamander and emerging from water onto land remains an amphibian-to-be and stays in its aquatic larval form. One probable cause of this arrested development is a lack of thyroxine, the hormone secreted by the thyroid gland; for if an axolotl is given thyroid gland extracted from cattle or iodine (an essential component of thyroxine) it turns into a salamander instead of living out its days as a full-grown juvenile, a Peter Pan whose problem is akin to that of humans with goiter. (In Wyoming and the Rocky Mountains, in fact, tiger salamanders often don't assume adult form and humans are liable to goiter, and the reason is lack of iodine in the water.) But it has also been suggested that the axolotl remains aquatic because the lakes it inhabits don't dry up, whereas the surrounding land—the axolotl being found wild only in certain lakes around Mexico City —is barren and dry. Life is easier, securer, in the lake; but, should the lakes dry up, the axolotl could still (I gather) change into a salamander, thus, it seems, having an option to which iodine is irrelevant. Further, an axolotl being transported to a laboratory or a dealer will change into an adult soon after having arrived!

So here is your axolotl, a full-grown juvenile able to breed, which doesn't grow up because either (1) its diet is incomplete or (2) it is programmed for survival, no matter what form it survives in or how incomplete its diet continues to be or (3) it's a bit sluggish and needs a jolt. How to reconcile these three explanations or evaluate them one against the others I don't know; but, clearly, in the axolotl the zoological spring fails to unwind, underwound by diet, overwound by exceptional caution, or just stuck. Just think: a bump equals a drought which equals iodine! And for all axolotls, who are surely better off, with their three chances, than sharks, which cannot easily stop and would sink if they did, and those species which have to get their vitamin C from outside sources. The self-protective axolotl (the name means "water sport" or "servant of water") does not go in search of what makes him develop until he's developed, which only iodine, or shocks ecological or transportational, can bring about. Small wonder that axolotls in aquaria spend most of their time on the bottom of the tank (cause or effect?) and when they muster enough energy to squabble can regenerate bitten-off gills, feet, and chunks of tail. Somebody up there has a soft spot for these stay-at-home amphibians *manqués,* and so too have the residents of Mexico City, who catch them to roast. What you yourself would do if you had one and he turned into a salamander because of a bump you'd given him (a highly probable occurrence), I can only half imagine; but he would almost certainly have to go, for axolotls keep easily while salamanders do not (and that is to ignore altogether their supposed passion for inhabiting fire).

Trying again, I come up with even more specialized flaws. The barracudina, for example, unlike most deep-sea fishes, has no light-emitting organs (most species of barracudina anyway) and so is in some difficulty swimming as fast as it does at depths of down to two miles. Its embarrassment, in the impersonally functional sense of being incommoded and handicapped, is surely worse than that of all hummels, those inexplicably hornless cattle and stags who nonetheless give a good account of themselves when competing with the horned; or of those species of army ants which, being averse to light, have to bore tunnels parallel to the march of the main body; or of those brown-lipped snails whose rim lips are white and those white-lipped snails whose rim lips are brown; or of hens that grow wattles, begin to crow, yet still lay an occasional egg; or of so-called "waltzing" mice, which have an abnormality of that part of the inner ear concerned with balance. Or consider such other samples as these of a partly mismanaged universe: the hereditary deafness found in white dogs like Dalmatians and bull terriers; *Gentiana acaulis,* which for reasons unknown refuses to flower in good soil but does well where the acid and lime counts are high; holly, whose greenish flowers are sometimes bisexual, although sometimes male and female flowers exist on *separate* plants (which is why they tell people to plant hollies in groups); uranium 235, old faithful of an unstable and vulnerable isotope which is as it is because it isn't otherwise ("We're here because we're here," they used to sing in World War One, rejoicing at minds gone blank); the particle for which, it seems, there is no anti-particle; flawed crystals in which one atom is where another should be or where no atom ought to be at all; the so-called incoherence of natural light, traveling as it does in brief packets of energy in random directions at uncorrelated times, compared with the light from an optical maser; acridines, believed to produce mutations which consist in the deletion or addition of a base or bases from the DNA chain. Such is the beginning of my list, over your head and before your time but nonetheless your alibi—not so much an excuse (the popular sense) as your being genuinely elsewhere while the universe put a foot wrong with that mouse or this crystal, but suffering a similar misadministration that relates you more closely than most people to Nature; a Nature I never really noticed until it bungled.

As a factory, Nature—the more familiar end of the universe—is more reliable than the best baseball pitcher ever, but less reliable than the London Underground. To be sure, where it falters it sometimes lowers its guard usefully: U-235 gives us the chain reaction, or at least the possibility of it; the misbehaving particle may teach us something about the "elementariness" of particles (e.g., are two different particles equally fundamental or is one merely an "excited" state of the other?). The imperfect crystal tells physicists a great deal about the mechanical properties of solids. And the deaf, or deaf because brain-damaged, child, from whom I wander only to hunt out some peers and analogues, is equally instructive. I mean, someone such as you would prepare anyone for the next phase, in which we find what I will call the superior intricacy of one deaf-blind child I know of: a child born without eyes or ears and with all internal organs so garbled that sex cannot be determined. Yet he/she knows how to get angry (why not?), is eager to sniff at things and people alike. Something on the lines of "Age 6—80 decibel hearing loss—IQ 75 on the Leiter International Performance Scale" says nothing much if you are willing to learn something more; neither does "Age 7—hearing nil—sight nil—sex?—IQ minimal" if you, and I mean other people as well as you, have a passion to learn (and that ambiguity I intend). How a parent himself proceeds from the statistics depends on who and what he is, how much of Nature he is willing to look at; but, pretty certainly, there will be some desperation in his proceeding. Which, given such standard desirables as warmth, light, and some health, may not be a bad thing. It's a bit like writing the prospective novel—being a prospector for fiction in uncharted areas—inasmuch as the parent doesn't know where he will end up or how.

To put it topically, locally: the parents run the home around the child; we around you. We learn your ignorances until they are ours. We steal your condition (steal *into* it) by means of risky analogies, like the mystic borrowing the lover's terms, the lover borrowing the mystic's. We glut you with smellables, tangibles, edibles, visibles: all the perfumes of Arabia; all the grades of sandpaper, leading up to a feel at an elephant; all the fluents from goat's milk to mercury; all the spices from cinnamon to chili; all the zoos, parades, Dufys, flags, unwanted *National Geographics,* French colonial stamps, travel posters, and rainbows we can muster. Always a color camera, preferably Polaroid, because you don't like to wait.

Against all this—your stark handicap and any voluptuously zany sharing in it—set a thought, neither apocalyptic nor original. Ten years after the atomic explosion on Bikini atoll, fishes were living in the trees and birds were sitting on sterile eggs; turtles, instead of going back to the sea after laying their own eggs, pressed on to the island's interior, where they died of thirst. Their skeletons remain, thousands of them, evidence of a gratuitous handicap we might have had the brains to do without. Speaking of brains, each brain having ten trillion cells of which most people bring only a fifth into play, I wonder how and when we shall be able to shift into dialogue and I can really (if you'll pardon the metaphor) bend your ear and no longer one-sidedly sound off into an interim that might last forever or, if it ends, end just short of enabling you to read these words. Even a serious brain injury can't kill off all ten trillion cells and an indefatigable effort can bring into action millions of cells that otherwise might never have been used at all. If the main highway is blocked off, we can try going through the side roads; which, surely, is why they were provided in the first place. (Or do they merely represent an inscrutable, pleonastic, French *ne?* I hope not.)

I find, anyway, an analogy which, although too picturesque to be medically proper, might appeal to you: water, so much a comfort to you that I sometimes think *you* amphibian, begins by following the original slopes and inequalities of whatever surface has newly formed or been upraised from the sea floor, but soon divides up into river systems, each river deepening and widening its valley as best it can—soft rock here, hard rock there; here a steep slope, there a shallow one; one river enlarging its drainage area at the expense of another in that slow but exciting-sounding maneuver called river capture. The rivers look after their own interests, and good for the rivers! At the end of the Ice Age, for example, when owing to the melting of ice from the St. Lawrence Valley the waters from the lakes flowed northeast again, the stream from Lake Erie plunged over the edge of a steep limestone escarpment, and, ever since, because of erosion, as a waterfall has cut its way further and further upstream. After the ice left the Baltic (we're traveling again), the Vistula and Oder rivers had a northward outlet and, in fact, broke through the line of the Baltic Heights. In Australia the waters of the Darling-Murray river system, slowing up as they reach the plains, deposit rock waste they no longer have the speed to carry; the beds and banks get higher and higher, and, in fact, in some places the rivers flow several feet above the level of the surrounding land. But flow they do, whereas the plateau of Mexico, from parts of which there is no outlet, abounds in saline depressions and great accumulations of debris.

There isn't *always* a way through; but, looking as I now am at two diagrams of drainage areas (before and after a shift of the Divide) which in a rudimentary way resemble drawings of the brain, I'll trust in Nature's capacity to change, in man's willingness to give Nature a helping hand. One river in Brazil has been made to flow upward; the Institute for the Achievement of Human Potential in Philadelphia floods brain-damaged children's senses with impressions, prescribes crawling in slatted boxes, eye exercises done with a flashlight, breathing masks to increase carbon-dioxide intake, minimum intake of liquids, and no music (for music stimulates the subdominant hemisphere of the brain). You yourself, like so many brain-damaged children (you may or may not be among these), were for years neither right- nor left-handed, a condition the Philadelphia patterning is meant to rectify—jogging Nature into going one way or the other (as it did when you began to use your left hand increasingly). This is to make Nature do what is within Nature's compass, whereas we can't, as far as I know, engineer the river of the mind uphill; the child who is psychotic or whose brain is defective—sickness or incompleteness—isn't handicapped but utterly disqualified.

You see, I'm getting classroomishly serious, not

laughing as often as you, in your ebulliently hectic way, would like—how abandoned you are when there is loud laughter you can hear and which you can join in. Behind those increasingly frequent neat and tender smiles of yours, you stockpile guffaws of an exquisite timbre that topple and mount at speed over a whole octave. You have taught us the virtue in play for play's sake and, as it were, have commandeered our senses, so that we hoard impressions and bits of offbeat information on your behalf, longing to tell you and hoping that, one day, we will.

Just because these things are so, and not otherwise, like U-235, we memorize the brown bear of the Arctic who eats female salmon only (for the succulent roe), the guillemot who on a narrow cliff ledge arranges its one egg heavy end inward; the bone needle, the size of a paper clip, and thirteen thousand years old, found twenty feet from where the Marmes Man's remains were uncovered in Washington State; the romantic-looking balconies which, jutting out over the canal from the weathered stone of the house walls in Guanajuato, Mexico, are really toilets built over an open sewer; triclad worms which live in the underparts of horseshoe crabs; sea pansies and sea wasps; the DNA of a pigmy virus created from inert chemicals; or, nearer your own stomping grounds, the published finding that autistic children are the only children who don't like school holidays (any more than you do, who always plead for "kool")—I know of one Oxford don's child who insists on crossing the Bodleian quadrangle in the same way time after time, into and out of the same two entrances. We're also saving for you the new center, in Pamplona of the bulls, for brain-damaged children; the deaf actors from Gallaudet College, Washington, D.C., performing Euripides' *Iphigenia in Aulis* with an eloquent wealth of hand movements which, one critic said, "seemed to chisel emotions out of the air"; a party of twelve deaf children who, traveling from Derby in England to Dortmund in Germany, were *en route* for almost twenty-four hours and, thanks to British Railways (who set up the itinerary), had to change trains five times; or, something in your future —although not for the born deaf, so I might rescript it—Exercise 35 in the Compound Consonant *dr* in a lip-reading primer: a surrealistic, sinister-bland non-conversation in which suburban propriety suffuses a Georgian hangover, with the only thing missing being a postilion struck dead, dumb, or deaf, by lightning. How's this?

Do you prefer *d*rama or farce?
*Dr*aw on your private bank account for the amount.
He *dr*ew out his savings and spent them.
Old Tom was a *dr*over in the early days.
What a *dr*eary prospect!
The roll of a *dr*um is stirring.
I think he's had a *dr*op too much.
We *dr*ank to their health and happiness.
Do we *dr*ess for dinner?
*Dr*ink to me only with thine eyes.
Is this a *dr*y area?
The *dr*ains need attention.
Some people *dr*own their sorrows in *dr*ink.

Drrrrr! It has, I think, to be deciphered like Linear B; but, clearly, if there is a hidden story, somebody blew his total pelf to sit in the first row at a happening in which an old shepherd called Drake (an ex-drummer) got so pixillated he fell in his best tuxedo down an open manhole and broke his neck on the encrusted geranium-tinted brick, there being no water to cushion his fall.

What I was getting ready to say, before I went off into a verbal equivalent of one of the sudden romps

Words for a Deaf Daughter

with which we rupture the days' even processes, was this: not only do you transform those close to you into Autolycuses, snappers-up of unconsidered trifles; you acquaint us, as much through what you miss as through what you discover, with the pageantry of life's incidentals: the texture of matters of fact, of the matter-of-fact. *Must tell Manda that*, we murmur but mostly we can't, unless there's a nonverbal way, lurid, preferably, and strong-smelling, with a surface rich in corrugations like the halved cabbages and an assertive taste. The sea, writes Rupert Brooke in one of his letters, "was �{squiggle}ᴺᴺᴺᴺ," which corrugation might not signify choppy (or whatever it did mean) to you, but resembles the mid-air scribble you do while asking for *kool* and, could you but transpose it from sea-green blackboard to wine-dark sea, would surely match how the British Channel felt to you the day you crossed by Condor Hydrofoil at about thirty-five knots from Jersey in the Channel Islands to Saint-Malo in France, your vulnerably white hands clamped on a rail and your face the color of porridge. And without being sick, on either the outward or the return trip, but gamely—with that stiff-lipped aghastness you reserve for the most trying trials in your trial-haunted childhood—tagging on while the cheap liquor that honor demands one buy was bought. *La belle France* was where you couldn't even muster the heart to sneer at an omelet.

But the bottle—ah, the bottle! GUARANTEED SAME QUALITY THROUGHOUT THE WORLD, it says just under the prancing boots of that jolly Regency buck (or whatever he is) in the red coat and the white drainpipes, himself sort-of-hydrofoiling a tenth of an inch above the blacklettered strip of Kilmarnock self-congratulation. I would guarantee *you* in the same terms, THROUGHOUT THE WORLD, not merely because one of your nicknames happens to be Proof, but because gold labels become you, as you have so often proved by affixing them to your forehead and arms with status-giving spit. And if, like this Scotch, you had been honored in Sydney in 1880, only a century after Captain Cook sailed along the green eastern coast of Australia, or in Paris in 1885 (4 triumphal arches to shelter under, one Eiffel Tower 985 feet high to gape at, millions of big umbrellas to sit and sip under), or in Jamaica in 1891 (from where I still remember the sordor and stench of French Town in Kingston, big landslides of molten chocolate in the crammed rain forests, Rastafarians with golliwog hair working in slow motion on the narrow hill roads, banked flowers on the university campus like a hundred gaudy burial mounds, drums at night out of the far trees while I bit on overcooked British mutton, hummingbirds frozen in midair)—if you had been there, if you had just *been,* you would surely have been By Appointment to Whatever Majesty it was that ruled the time: court jester extraordinary, mistress of the royal sausage rolls, keeper-finder-polisher-tester of all Majestical ear trumpets. Or, given chance, you would have been Ludwig van Beethoven's bedmaker (he being the one who, in his Heiligenstadt Testament, furiously confessed, "I must live like an exile," though I reckon what he called his "fiery, impulsive temperament, sensible, even, to the distractions of social life" had nothing on yours; after six years of deafness, both you and he, you at six and he at twenty-eight, are level. "Compelled early in my life," he cries, "to isolate myself, to spend my life in solitude. . . . Already in my 28th year I have been compelled to become a philosopher; this is no easy matter").

Already, he says. As you already know, and as I myself realize from those bleak, expressionless faces you sometimes wear—confronting yourself with something you don't know as a hurt or a riddle but which doesn't feel right—there's an answer we cannot find to a question you can't formulate: *Must it be?* The whys and wherefores belong to a Sphinx whom we, reversing the Greek myth, would strangle for riddling with us in the first place. Clever Oedipus, recognizing man as the being which, "having only one voice, has sometimes two feet, sometimes three, and sometimes four and is weakest when it has most," clever Oedipus got the Sphinx to throw herself to death; but, confronted with a being which, having only one voice, has sometimes two ears, sometimes four, and is weakest when it is spoken to, might never have won the prize of the Theban throne. Answering right, he earned the right to stick Jocasta's pin into his eyes; answering wrong, he would have been strangled by the Sphinx on her rock. Either way, a setup: no quarter given, none asked; no buddy spared even a dime, none panhandled for. If there is a quick way to Colonus, where Oedipus spent his last hours under the favorable auspices of the Eumenides, we never hear of it. Art, for the Victorians, was the quickest way out of Manchester; but there is no quick way with the riddle of your handicap. I see you in a portable ghetto you carry round with you, the only inhabitant, and sometimes—when busyness and distractions and horseplay fail and you submit to the pure silence of your birthright—you are as forlorn as Beethoven pleading, one month before his death, for "old, white Rhine or Moselle wine." His bottles, Rüdesheimer Berg, 1806, arrived two days before his death. As the Abbé Stadler said when blessing him the year before, *"Hilft's nix, schadt's nix"* (Does no good, does no harm)—so let's talk our way back to our own bottles. Complaining might do harm; does no good.

The last of the "Highest Awards" the Scotch won—or so it seems from the gold label—was Brisbane in 1897. Nothing in our own century? *Nothing?* Skip it, here's the Wolfschmidt vodka (70 Proof in Britain, 80 in the States) which came in a tiny *sabot* from a creaky dark wineshop in St. Helier, an unfancy bottle but having a label resplendent with tiny gold medallions (thirty-four overlapping like grape bunches), two coats of arms with, beneath one, in minuscules, MOSCOW plus indecipherable date, and, beneath the other, NOVGOROD (I think) plus an equally indecipherable date. It also says "Original Genuine Vodka since 1847." Before Scotch, that is, which has congeners in it, whereas vodka hasn't. Packed into the small rear label in the tiny print you're always supposed to read in contracts and insurance policies, there's a roll call of cities (or towns) where Wolfschmidt has won *diplômes d'honneur* and medals that are bronze, silver, or gold (a bibulous Olympics): just imagine, all this ritual delectable bibbing wove its way in between the wars and the earthquakes and the plagues, all the way from the year in which Grant became President (1869) while they were disestablishing the Irish Church and opening formally the Suez Canal, to the year (Berne, 1954) when, at Bikini atoll, the first American hydrogen bomb went off, messing up the animal and bird life there (as we've said), and food rationing ended in Britain and I, back from Columbia University, began my military service in a coarse blue battledress (gear for peace) that chafed the inside of my thighs. Good old Wolfschmidt, whose honor roll of places-won-at would have delighted Marlowe's Tamburlaine himself and twice, anyway, won appointment to the Imperial House of Romanoff. *Romanoff?* Off—

Off we go, here we go, round and into and through the year, no years, YEAR-Z, 1869-70, ST. PETERSBURG! the Russian one, where Peter the Great issued a ukase ordering his entire court to learn to dance and where Nijinsky, in 1900, was chosen for the Imperial School because he had extraordinary thighs. St. Petersburg, *Peters———burg!*

Bur, you say, evoking the female hop catkin, some person who can't be shaken off, *burr,* a winter shiver, *brr.* Let's try the next vodka victory, nearer your mouth. The clearing house of the world, London. *Lon ———don.*

Lon, you whisper. I'll add Chaney, both of whose parents were deaf, which is how he learned to mime.

Now Riga, ice-blocked in winter (isn't it?): *Ree. Ga. Ree! Drr, drr,* you made a thin, cold sound, like an icicle going up a silver-tongued mockingbird's nostril!

Vienna, a big wheel, round and round, roundabout.

You say it without hesitating. *Roundabou. Roun.*

Vienna, I tell you. *Vee. Enn.*

Ben, percussively. *Ben, ben.*

Benissimo. Try Jelgava, on the river Aa—you pick up the last word and give it full voice, your own special sound for histrionic pity when one or the other of us nicks his finger or you've rammed the umbrella spike into our tender zones and the urgent, pretend cables go out to—oh, where?—Karachi, Tokyo, Timbuctoo: WOUNDED IN FRONT AGAIN, which is where James Boswell said one *should* have been wounded to be a man at all. What? Oh, nothing. Try Paris. PAR—— EE.

And, of course, effortlessly as this making you a present of my own mentality, you come out with *EE,* meaning "Please forgive me that hostile act, we are friends and playmates and henchmen again, aren't we, you *will* be around for me to do it to again?" *EE?* My girl, there's no right speech out of Paris town, which Frankie Villon, a pop singer from way back, said against the chill wind of his luck: arguing his case for staying there, see, in spite of burglaries and thefts and jail and two near hangings until it took a whole Parliament to banish him, the rascal with snow on the brain. Whereas Moscow, where, wouldn't you know it? they serve iced drinks and ivory ice cream in the railway station on the most freezing nights and nothing else; Moscow's an immovable feast, and I don't here give a damn about the mute *e* so long as we don't get a mute you. *Moss*——*Go*.

And you say Mo, as in Moses.

Try Bordeaux, on all those bottles of mine you like to paw.

Beau, you seem to say, uttering good and valid and pertinent French which is utterly beautiful except you mean "escalator." So let's go on to Naples, where Lady Hamilton, espying Nelson come all the way from Alexandria in the shattered *Vanguard,* yelled, "O God! Is it possible!" and fell into his arms in a faint. NAY— —PL.

You agree with me and say your *Nay*.

Amsterdam! Where, for breakfast, they eat strawberry sandwiches! OM-STER-DOM. Said with a king-sized strawberry in the mouth. OM-STER-DOMM.

Om, you say, half of Omsk, which is not on the list of vodka triumphs.

Grazie, try Nice, amber and ultramarine and bony, sunny white, klaxons and Caravelles and whipping rainbow pennants. Dufy. NEECE. And, lo and untold, you have it perfectly, needling the vowel and surreptitiously tapping your tongue against the sibilant. *Neece, th.* And so, regarding ANTWERP LIVERPOOL EDINBURGH BRUSSELS TIFLIS CHICAGO, all those illustr—

oops, *gung,* your plastic Hong Kong hammer in my eye, gosh—*illustrious*. I said it. *Cities*. I got it out. Half the conetents—ha, leave it, I like the idea of *cone*tents however accidentally come by—of this house come from Hong Kong, where typhoons almost but not quite float out to sea those thousands of sweat-laboring human snails who assemble all that gaudy, therapeutic, polythene trash in overgrown kennels flung and stuck on the sides of the hills many social niches below, but uphill-toiling niches above, Kai Man Book Store and Wah Kiu STUDIO, classy ports of call for you know who—

You know Hoo?
Hoo who?
Hoo Flung.
Hoo Flung What? That celluloid mallet into my eye, all that already caking plaster of Paris against the outside of the kitchen window; maybe some Optine will help both. Let's have a song, girl; a song, girl, while we wait for normal vision to resume:

> You've two big teeth,
> You've two big teeth
> Right up there in the front,
> And spanking chopping new,
> But no teeth at the side.

Don't ever, please, wrench off bottle caps with those. *Eeeee*.

And so—no, that's too conciliatory a transition. Better to say: Now, about the oval-framed blue-tinted passport picture of Marie Brizard on the Cherry Brandy from Bordeaux (*Marie Brizard et Roger,* it says actually, but Roger is not, as they say, in evidence). Two clumps of cherries on the label seem to be held in space by a complex of goldwire curlicues resembling treble clefs on their sides, like inebriated signatures. 24° it says to their left, 70 cl. to their right. *Maison fondée en 1755,* before vodka, before Scotch, *hein?* and, on the aluminum cap, DEVISSEZ three times, which is roughly what *you* mean when you say "wind" when applied to clocks, or, by extension, to peeling the black masking paper off a Polaroid photograph. So: you wind—unwind—the top, snapping these seven threads of frail metal but only, if we believe the arrows, counterclockwise. If you go with the clock, you screw home the cap for all eternity and the only way in is to smash the bottle with your favorite length of iron piping. You love, I know, the raised lettering in the bottle's glass, running your fingers over it like Braille, and with the same humming hoot that gives you away when, after maximum logistical stealth, you have filched and opened a flip-top can of beer and are pouring onto the ice cubes in your tumbler a cold, golden, quick one such as you always take in the kitchen, your own version of a *distingué*. One cube in your mouth cools the froth as it lingers after the beer has gone, and the can ring goes on your finger, the wedge-shaped metal flap being the precious stone. Or semi-precious stone. Or semi-precious talisman.

Your actual birthstone, my *Executive's Data Book* tells me, happens to be opal or tourmaline, from Latin *opalus* from Sanskrit *upala,* which is for "gem," and from Singhalese *toramalli* (what next?). One is "hydrous silica" with sometimes changing colors: milk-white or bluish with greens, yellows, reds, while the other is a mineral of various colors, comes out of granite, and has "electric properties." I sometimes think that if you asked all the questions I imagine you might if things were otherwise we'd go into the dictionary and never come out: live in there, I mean, hitching our way from word to word as if words were inns and explaining ourselves with *Oh, we're fun-ologists* (like Marilyn Monroe saying, *I'm a chant-ooze*), and all the time hunting derivations down through cognate forms and guessing Scotch-Vodka-Marie Brizard guesses when it said [?] or "etym. dub." Why, we'd even find out why Sanskrit's called Sanskrit and Singhalese Singhalese; and, who knows, Etym. Dub. would keep us fairly constant company like a worldly wise, cautious great white hunter until he went off with [?] or was supplanted by Erron. Flynn or Sl. (Slim the Trim Gun) or Unexpl. (which is a word with a *pl* in it, which is plane to you, which proves you can harbor a Boeing or a VC-10 in a very small, unnoticed, suffix of a hangar indeed). *Pl!* you call, as if to friends, as they bluster over in their tunnel-throated landing approaches, wheels down and all lights winking in the daylight. And then you go on with your household chores at the sink or on the grass: either washing the alarm clocks in a deep detergent foam with a stiff brush, stacking plates with maenad abandon (tossing each one from you at least two feet with nerve-testing crashes you don't hear), and shampooing the fire irons, poker, tongs, hearth brush and all; or brushing the grass, weeding the garden by up-rooting all the genuine flowers, and jumping up and down in the garbage cans to pack things tight.

To please you (because we draw with our fiber or felt pens on the same rough surface), I'm writing this on the insides of the larger envelopes that arrived in the mail, containing catalogues from Blackwell's and the college departments of eager publishing houses: one long slit, then a short, and we have an approximately quarto sheet on which to draw slides, baths, planes and even such bizarre things as words and, always, unless we are playing truant by tinkering with Japanese, spelling in the Initial Teaching Alphabet. *Wauk, doent run.* Or, maybe, instead of either, *Fly!* I see you've already helped yourself to the picture, in yesterday's newspaper, of E.S. Kraus's 250-seat airbus whose fuselage is shaped like a trout and the Hindenburg and R 100 airships (rather than the cylindrical Zeppelins of World War One). It reminds me of Crescent II, the little glider I designed when I was fourteen and submitted, as plans, to the *Aeromodeller:* my first publication, bringing my first check. "This glider," the Unabashed Young Designer noted in the bottom corner of the gratuitiously intricate drawing, "is for free soaring flight only and flies fast—will hold thermals. Performance: 1st, 24 secs, 2nd, 31 secs, 3rd, 32.5," and up and up until sublime anoxia cancels all. It was wartime, so for certain parts (except the trim tab) I specified copper instead of aluminum, this being unobtainable because, as Spitfires, it was demolishing the Nazi formations over our heads, or, as Lancasters, plastering German cities with ten-ton bombs that converted them into something less than the ash on a Churchill cigar. In the sky the aluminum saucepans of yesterday found a lasting incarnation. Or in wreckage in dank fields and through the roofs of cowsheds and among the small shops of cities, subjected to a final scorch beyond all heat of cooking, and with men in them.

A good saucepan outlives any of us, doesn't it? Whereas even a good plane doesn't, and, nowadays, is obsolescent after five years, finished after ten. The longest lasters, I suppose, have been the Avro Ansons (in some of which I toured around above the British Isles, once dramatically identifying Cambridge as North London) and the DC3's: thirty years apiece, which sounds impossibly dogged in times when the Navy, in the TV guides, proclaims "Our New Navy's All Muscle And It Needs Men! Missiles That Punch Aircraft Out Of The Sky . . . Cut The Coupon. You Can Join At Fifteen." In return you get a fifty-two-page booklet that woos even further all young Nelsons and John Paul Joneses whose chins are pimply. In these days the gun barrel goes up with the projectile, the horn accompanies its own seed. . . . Sorry, this is out of your ken so far, although I know the boys at school ascend the lavatory partitions to watch you girls. Let's just agree that we don't want *any* aircraft punched out of the sky, and risk the death-delivering ones. Death? Oh, I'll save a postscript for it; a blank thing, it blanks us out, and there are some things which, along with William Ralph Inge, "the gloomy Dean," I "could not bring myself to say in English . . . about our little girl" (instead, on the loss of his daughter, he wrote verses in Latin). Or, for that matter, bring myself to say *to* you who have, even if you don't know it, known one death in the family.

Strange, though: out of some preternatural tact, you do not grieve over absences; you accept. You have no metaphysics, no cosmic worries, but just an assumption of your own shrill perpetuality, a busy insouciance that's near-Olympian. When a leper's thumb fell into his bowl, the Buddha ate it—and that's your sort of conduct too; you retrieve and immediately munch all of your food that falls and all—carpet whiskers, fluff, dirt, cigarette ash—that comes with it. Except (there are so many yous) you'll never touch cheese, chocolate, or fish (saving only the humble brisling in tomato sauce and the smallest shrimps).

Where, I keep saying, where were we? Having already communicated our personalities to each other (a loving tug-of-peace both raucous and casual), we fumble when in words. Too much to tell you all at once and I can't say it all out in one word, much as I would like to. Silence may be golden and older, closer to Eden, than speech; but *our* near-silence lasts too long. I'm all for an age of silver in which, wearing the vowels down, we open our bird's-eyes, view the last third of this century, and then happily slither over the edge into yapping decadence: all wings clipped from young chickens since modern breeds of poultry never fly and they're easier to pack that way; all sculpture done in plastic tubing; all music tape-recorded in aviaries; all painting done in mine-dark rooms; all writing done by verbal roulette; all talk by reading thoughts; all procreation by registered test tube; all leisure psychedelic and not feet-up lazy; all human odor vanquished by on-squirted processed musk of animals; all tobacco mentholated; all rivers stale with inspissated industrial filth; all sunlight held off by the atmosphere; all buffalo, otter, and bald eagles extinct; all roads jammed with stationary, unmovable, and rust-ing cars; all coffee and wheat burned to raise the price, and all hogs buried; all food in cans stacked under dead fields in colossal silos; all disease and dying done away with and the healthy crammed fifty to a room while the fallout flakes endlessly down; all breath taking suspended until the success of the project to abolish saliva. . . . Apropos of nothing—almost but not quite—did you know that Robinson Crusoe's real name was Kreutznaer? He tells us in his second sentence.

But enough of him; I am told how a few days ago you set the school on its ear by mounting your A1 De Luxe Pullman Top Person Jetstream squeal in the playground. A button was missing from your new nylon blouse and you sustained the siren of your SOS until the matron found a replacement and sewed it in place. At once you fell quiet, beamed, and they all—matron, your teacher, and her assistant—felt they had been released from some monstrous visitation which nonetheless carried within it the germ of an amnesty. Could such an awful keening have been emitted by this same genial, poised, smiling face? Only that morning, your teacher and the other children in your class had been admiring your new blue-and-white outfit; pretty, they said, *pre'ee,* so the loss of a button hit you doubly hard.

You surprise only those people for whom your bravura neatness (in some things) isn't an accepted part of day-to-day living. Your socks must be, literally, up tight, with no disfiguring wrinkles or twists, and the tops must be folded down exactly the right amount. Two hair clips on one side of your head must have counterparts in identical position on the other side, holding your hair in the same degree of tension. The same goes for hair ribbons, which must bind punitively, and for the rubber bands under them, which must never snap; for you know the difference at once, no matter how tight the ribbon stays over the break. Curtains open or closed must match. When one of us lifts a cup or takes off a shoe or a slipper, so do you. When one of us crosses legs, so do you, and with the same leg uppermost (you watch only one at a time, otherwise your legs would be like windmills while you tried to fit all positions into one ensemble). When we eat, it is perilous to set down all the tools at once: you abominate unclean platters, tools not in action, and, given a chance, remove them to the kitchen forthwith, heedless of pauses for breath or rest. Given your own way, you would clear the table before the meal began; one brief glimpse of a hissing steak, one sniff of steaming vegetables, and you would clear the decks. Sometimes, even, when you are especially enraged or merely want to be extra-emphatic, you remove plate and uneaten portion in one fluent dispatch to the garbage can outside. At all costs be tidy (Kreutznaer-Crusoe was, too): except that you yourself dawdle over most of your meals and, in the evenings especially, lie flat on the carpet or pedal your legs in the air while your slippers dangle by their heels from your toes. Something Roman wins out in you eventually, so that you trough in indolent disregard of whatever clothes you have on: marinara sauce is the insignia most usually to be found on your blouses; butter in your hair, oil along your arms, bits of ham in your shoes, and, as often as not, your plate and the knife you use as a spoon (if you aren't eating with your hands) are marooned in a pool of milk.

Gobbling or nibbling, you preposterously feed both of the girls within you: the precisionist and the hooligan, the one creating exquisite designs for the other to wreck, the other manufacturing a chaos which the precisionist is tempted to remedy until the very last moment, when she chickens out. Only special untidinesses bother you; all others you ignore. I sometimes think you would happily live in ankle-deep mud so long as your stocking tops showed straight above the surface and your hair was lashed tight, with nothing straying.

So, we tell your teacher, if certain treasures break, repair at once with anything at hand: Scotch tape, chewing gum, stamp edging. Or be prepared to have both eardrums bombarded into singing numbness by the most belligerent plea in the world: *Oi-ya!* For that is the kind of girl you are. A banshee-mandrake lurks behind your substantial, protein-glowing beauty, ever ready to coerce the world into righting tiny errors in arrangment, even when, say, you are in a mood of gracious repose with your legs spread wide before a winter fire to warm your vitals. *Cuishing,* the Manx call it, having a *cuish;* and that's part of your birthright too. Your blood runs faster with the heat from the fire and fuels your vocal organs until, I think, you could rival the howl of a gale off that Irish sea in a bad March. But summer heat knocks you out, driving you to quite voluntary siestas on your bed or, on torrid days, into moments of amok brandishing of sharp things followed by an almost catatonic hour or two, during which the heat seems to possess and annul you as no freeze of winter can. Cold, I gather, you almost enjoy although it insults your ears and chest; heat you loathe and must be sheltered from.

But whatever the protective garb—anorak or straw hat in the Caribbean style—it has to be colorful and chic, a touch *outré* perhaps, and this is clearest when you choose in stores with that unfailing eye for the most expensive item and the newest mode. And whatever is can be made more so with badges, the lions and castle of Saint-Malo, the three-legged Manx swastika, the Penn State mountain lion, to all three of which we must be adding an Oxford ox and, those family arms you gain on your mother's side, the dove with olive branch and the comprehensive-sounding phrase, *deus et pax.*

So you'll never have to have your line researched to see if you're entitled to a family crest or need to transact with that old Air Force colleague of mine who, when last heard of, was selling coats of arms to American tourists under the title of herald *poursuivant,* with letters patent as befitted him and a set of red silk doctoral robes for an honorary degree he'd somehow omitted to acquire. We sympathize, don't we? with his helpless desire for pageantry, for the gorgeous. We come into the world, *out of mother,* as a child wrote in a poem I read somewhere, *and a giant smacks us.* Who, after that, if he could remember it, wouldn't want to be a peacock in a splendid wrapper?

3.

Birds

Cuffed or overreaching from some rain spout choked with leaves, mold, rust, and the caked soot of industrial fallout, one fledgling sparrow hit the concrete, lightly as a balled-up Kleenex:
 a weathered-looking thing, mousy and mudthumbed, pessimistic black match-head eyes saying *fnint, fnint,*
 puny chirp, clover-soft claws like commas on the ends of the leatherette leg stems,
 and tuft wings only.
 So you took it, him, her, in and coaxed the wildness out of (let's say) him, versed him in your wordless way in plate-rim perching, on-your-shoulder standing, inside-your-blouse-hiding against the unspoiled skin which, at first, goose-pimpled at his touch. Unabashed, he reconnoitered the house, shelves and pelmets and all the undusted places, and flipped tiny pellets of meat eater's lime behind him as he went. He soon lost his cuffed-out look and delivered regular morning huzzas with a baby-avian accent. Knew where his meal ticket was, troughed on wriggling mealworms specially procured. But was not averse to minced steak, a flake of ham, a tiny strip of nerveless clipped-off cuticle, or— as I discover from his kind in general as they infest the lawn day after day—the carcass of a roasted chicken with parsley-sage stuffing smudged against the transparent bones of what's left. Go he had to, rejoining his squadron through an upper downstairs window,

Goliath-strong, Alice-innocent, Thumbelina-unreal. And never came back or tried to, thus leaving a gap behind him for the bird in your life, a gap we have filled so far with two successive specimens of *Melopsittacus undulatus*, these being budgerigars first-named Orry I and II after a mythical Gaelic king, but whom you dub *boid* and who thus has become *Boyd*, a real name to drop in company. Boyd I survived a week only; the vet yanked his neck hard and blood spilled, then seeped, from the beak. Boyd II you knew wasn't Boyd I, and you stared at him with all the squinting gravity of a tourist being conned in a bazaar but not really knowing how to counter. You saw the same iridescent green, yes; the same flimsy egg-shaped trunk, the same parsonically clownish face, the same cage. But you held back, no doubt in the belief that he who marks time knows it the second time round: no plucking at the Chagall-blue tail feathers, no cupped hand around the plump nothing of his belly with your elbow resting on the wire drawbridge of the cage door; no flicks at the dowel and wire swing suspended from the inside of the top of the cage. And, for a time, you didn't even offer to clean out the tray in the bottom.

Need finally ousted memory as it usually does if we talk to you with exaggerated hand gestures and the Three Stooges faces that are standard in this house— all for the purpose of distracting you until you concentrate on what you actually need and not on what you used to have. They say Nijinsky was built like a bird and had webbed feet, which is why he could jump so high, stay up there as long as it takes to blow a nose. *Tell you anything so long as you know you are being talked to.* And so, with Boyd II in mind, we go, go, go: *TELL ME TELL ME TELL ME!* OI-YA O-O-I-I—YA! *TELLTELLTELL!*

This is a four-guinea orange slubbed Cecil Gee roll-neck shirt which I'm wearing, an export special. STOP-STOP? HOW *can* I STOP?

An old Good-King-Wenceslas, King-Lear-Canute-type statue has been removed from the Palace of Westminster and is for sale along with his neighbors the gryphons and unicorns and a queen fidgeting with the Anston stone braid of her robe and a praying other king (Edward the Confessor?) whose hands are drooping low. Want a statue for the garden, a soap box for bird orators, an outsize peg to hang a balloon on? STOP

What if Nosferatu met Robinson Crusoe-Kreutznaer? Alone, the pair of them, on an island, hungry and mighty irritable? STOP OI-YA OI-YA STOP

They've just dynamited the Most Beautiful Hotel In The World, the Royal Picardy at Le Touquet, the hotel with the aerated water in its pool and having its own airport STOP OI-YA

Palomar astronomers are studying a radio source called 3C9 receding at four-fifths the speed of light and already nine billion light years away: almost a light year for each cell, used or unused, in your brain STOP

In Micronesia, as soon as a boy child is born, they plant coconut trees for him; and boy and trees grow up together, and they keep him in food and drink, liquor and skin lotion, buttons, butter, slippers, soap, rope and rugs, plastic and pickles, thread and timber. He drinks the sun and inhales the moon and does not know he lives on an island perched on the summit of a submerged mountain as high as Everest, an island propped up into the air by the accumulated skeletons of tiny sea creatures STOP OI—STOP

There is, going into the Congo, soap collected by Quakers from Philadelphia hotels STOP OI-YA YA YA YA YA YA!

The Viet Cong give reporters souvenirs in the form

of aluminum combs made from shot-down American planes STOP   OOOOOIII-YAH!

In Florida, Greek sponge divers who get the bends are packed in ice STOP

Someone claims to have seen Don Quixote on Wall Street STOP

Blind, Frederick Delius was carried in his chair to the top of a hill so he could feel the dawn STOP

Someone says a white polar bear once quoted Virgil STOP

Al-Siyuti, never mind who, tells how Zubaydah, alias Creamkin, once crammed a poet's mouth with jewels which he sold for twenty thousand dinars STOP

One apprentice bull fighter, a *novillero,* keeps a whole ham hanging in his Mercedes and in his private plane to remind him of his early poverty STOP

In A.D. 700, passengers sailing to Byzantium were forbidden to fry fish STOP

Sigurd the Volsung scalded his fingers with boiling blood and thrust them into his mouth to cool; as soon as the blood touched his tongue he understood the language of birds STOP

Boa constrictor is tough eating, grain-fed rats are tasty, iguanas suit those whose stomachs "soar above all prejudices" (Charles Darwin said it), giant tortoises STOP STOP

You are beginning to scream *Eeeeeeeeeeeeeeeee,* it is still the wrong bird, not the wrong topic or set of gestures, not the weather or your stomach or even the ragged trim of your socks or the bent Space Patrol sugar cigarette stranded between the fingers of your left hand, *oi-ya, eeeeeeeee,* it is just the wrong one out of all the grass parakeets in the world. Call them what we will—Australian lovebirds or *melo*-etcetera—this is the one one you don't want. Something-instead-of-a-sparrow you took, although with your own patented sick-grinning bad grace that says how let-down and foul you'd feel even if things were suddenly to come right. But a changeling demolishes the steady frieze you count upon and maybe even implies loathsome finalities beyond, say, the last of today's ice cream, the ball-point gone dry and having to be thrown away because it isn't designed for a refill, the apple core upon which you cannot graft the crisp flesh again. Mini-ends, these, which you heed with eyes as calibrating as a gunsmith's. It would be the same if you'd had a Biscay bull or a lava lizard. You would prefer, I reckon, to lick the same popsicle day in, day out, if only one would last that long—the same steak, the same loaf, the identical gob of mustard; all your paintings on the same sheet of paper, all baths with the same cake of soap, all rest with the same sleep, all EEEEEE*eeeeeee*eeeee—eee- eee- (ee): your scream has diminished into a plaintive hoot.

Boyd irrevocably is the generic specific particular, the one word for that *boid*. I'll bite my tongue, but that won't alter the facts of succession for you, who want—oh, complicatedly perverse and sly desire—a static, monist universe in whose laundry sameness you have a perfect place provided you yourself don't change. Henry James's "special radiance of disconnection" has no appeal to you; instead, you want a special radiance of supreme forms—graffiti in the margins of Genesis which no hack with mop and pail can efface and no after-hours renegade numen modify. Your vocabulary has no plurals, so you're entitled, aren't you, to your brash, ecstatic singularity which requires all birds to be one and the same? I watch a jet through the window that curls and flexes like a worm as it moves past a flaw in the glass and then resumes its shape again, never having changed at all. I'm glad *you* didn't see it, because, of that phenomenon, there is absolutely no explaining I could offer you. Time out now, just a few minutes.

There arrived in the mail the other day a book containing studies of such children as you (you undiffidently, as usual, thought the package was for you, and in a profound sense it was). One contribution is by one of the medical men who tried to diagnose you, and he says, "After experience" (as the poet W. D. Snodgrass would put it), "preoccupation with tried and familiar things and repetition of stereotyped pieces of behaviour brings and maintains relief from anxiety at the expense of progress in learning and adaptation." *Wow,* you say, *what on earth*—but he did see how you clung to and clamored for the miniature bath. What he says bears also on this refusal of the second budgerigar and, I think, on its refined converse in your attitude to a discarded, very elegant black umbrella of your mother's which has a loose spike I have attached by means of a short, tapered inch of hexagonal pencil fitted through it. Every day you pull off the spike and bring it to me, along with the big screwdriver and the claw hammer, to have it reaffixed, thus maintaining the umbrella in a state of permanent intermittent disrepair. The only thing you can do about one bird's succeeding another is to adjust mentally, which you sometimes find as easy as opening up a pharaoh's tomb with a pin, whereas the umbrella—umbrellas being time-honored objects in your defensive anthology of the world—you can take liberties with, playing fast and loose with it against the certainty of its never becoming like Humpty Dumpty. You modify its condition only to reassert its durable identity (like a tiny Maud Bodkin with an archetypal pattern). And when, after some puzzling and some crude handiwork with a penknife, I plug the spike back on, you hold the umbrella vertical before you, shivering with an ecstasy we all might envy and chanting, with an awestruck lilt, *brella, brella, brella!* The Holy Grail, the Shield of Achilles, the brand Excalibur coming up out of the lake could give no greater joy, no more captivating a glimpse of the reticent *Logos,* than this contraption of torn water-proofed cloth and disintegrating stays. You hang it, dead center, with patient accuracy, on the crossbar of the hanger holding a suit, an offering infinitely more pleasing to me than the links of raw sausage you once habitually hung in the same spot.

You impress me, for not only do you now try to repair the umbrella yourself on this very desk I'm at, hammering and puffing and scraping with the knife and then squinting down the shaft like a billiards player with a faulty cue; you have even reconciled yourself to Boyd II who, I agree, is less tame and less intimately sociable than his predecessor. Sit on your shoulder like the sparrow and Boyd I? Not he. At most, when you rest your hand on one of the four perches flimsily installed in his cage, he'll set a claw on your knuckles, and you, you hold your breath impossibly long. Big exhalation, then, which ruffles his green fluff but not enough to make him shift his claw. He doesn't—

I'm sorry, I've forgotten what: a nicely spoken lady has just been at the door offering, as "a member of a group representing all religions" (*all?*), to discuss, of all things, religion: that which *binds,* hey? Honk, honk. Madam, if the Lulu were at home and not elsewhere pursuing her studies in ballistics, boys, and the breast stroke, I would have you in to wrestle like Job with her: best of three falls, Rabelaisian angel *versus* proselytizer; one of God's sports *versus* one of God's PR itinerants; handicap *versus* the Light of the World. There are in this lighted world so very many beautifully spoken ladies whose only handicap is an unmanured gentility gleaned from taste, good books, and a nice upbringing. Faith, they preach, some of them, and even more of them culture. Some of them, having no knowledge, counsel. Some of them, because they hate the body, become—ironic term—mistresses in girls' schools. And there are gentlemen who, lacking gentleness and gentility as well as a passable intellect, discover an outlet for their malevolence among young males. One such, at my old school, had to be sacked for breaking a meter rule across the spine of a boy prone on a table in an empty staff room. Another such, headmaster of the same school, went from my mind altogether after I left his vicinity but recrudesced, when I was twenty and entering Oxford, with a character assassination addressed to the rector of my college-to-be; who read it aloud to me, grinned, and tore it up. A doctor of divinity and therefore exceptionally equipped for dealing with rowdy teenagers in an undistinguished secondary school, he had also been severely gassed in World War One (in which my father lost his left eye and almost the right). San Quentin, we said in our callous way, would have made a better job of things; but, surviving as he did, this quasi-hieratic *Gauleiter* of Divinity in a gown that reeked of mothballs and putrescent kipper, developed remarkable expertise in what I call distributing the shit.

Still a bit of anger left, you see! How anyone can enjoy school I do not know, not when that's how they treat some of the non-handicapped in some of the places. You, I'm sure, will fare much better; it takes a lot of selfless dedication to teach in such a school as yours, where the important thing is not rigmarole and parroting and punishment, but the human potential of individual children who, some of them, may never be able to speak conventionally as long as they live. Your teachers are the sort of people who are grateful for what can be, not the sort who specialize in being petulant about what cannot.

O.K.: end of extra-curricular seminar; back to faith and culture, one excellent test of which is to help you up the stairs while cupping with one hand (so it won't fall and like soft oil paint smear stockings, shoes, rug) the Polish boiling sausage which you have involuntarily shifted into your blue school panties. Always, when you, child of Nature, squat while playing, atavistic habit has a chance of taking over. I have seen you take the delicious—because deliberate—liberty of flooding your slide from the top platform just as if you were a grizzled prospector in the Sierra Madre sluicing for gold. And then, all conscience and giggling regret, you fetch bucket and mop and swab the full length of the metal runway with hot water and a foaming cleanser, having restaked your claim with a picric libation.

But the excremental's only the beginning, isn't it? The freshman bit. Later courses in faith and culture would entail trying to explain to you why we, against whose ears you sometimes thrust your rattling alarm clocks, never wear hearing aids; where anywhere is; what money is; what a surname is for; which day is which by date; that you will grow into a woman; and what God is reckoned to be by people who, through argument or ritualistic fawning, would "save" you. I quote from the 1838 annual report of the Ulster Institution for the Deaf and Dumb and the Blind, Belfast:

> A little mute, in his 8th year, a day scholar, was unfortunately killed at one of the Factories before he could have known the revealed will of God. Very different, however, were the circumstances of a poor blind boy, who died about the same age. He was delicate and deformed; but during a lingering and painful illness he discovered a vigour of mind, an eagerness for spiritual instruction, a meekness of disposition, which gave satisfactory evidence of a saving change of heart.

"an 'earth-ecstatic' . . ."

Kindly do not be meek, that's all I ask of you. At school assembly, which is gratifyingly casual, those who are present clap hands above their heads; the fun supplication I call it when I'm not, as sometimes, brooding on the variously handicapped giving thanks for incapacities that render them immune to theological coercion or asking for apocalyptic favors. No, your own ebullient joy in being alive makes you, in one of Edna St. Vincent Millay's better phrases, an "earth-ecstatic," pleased by your own hallucinations (Fred, say, or when you look down to where the wall meets the floor and delightedly shout *ice, ice!*) and asking pitifully little out of life—although that little, being specially and unvaryingly eclectic, wears out those around you.

I've drawn for you, and cut out with scissors, I don't know how many baths and slides; finishing one is the best reason for doing another.

The French psychologist Zazzo has pointed out—and with the force of a revelation because no one before him had thought about so obvious a fact—that children such as you, being slow to progress scholastically, often tend to be at a particular stage longer than other children and therefore become reluctant to move on even when they are ready for it mentally. They don't want to do the necessary unlearning, exchange life belt for water wings and these for scuba outfit, and so on. That you recently did so, graduating from kindergarten to junior school with none of the tumult we expected, but with elated voracity, is a small marvel—brought about in part by your first teacher, whose sympathetic determination won you over and made you learn. Her name you still don't know, any more than you know the names of the children in your new class; but her face and general appearance you flung yourself toward with plunging affection. Say her name here: Mrs. Standeven, the name itself like an allegorical promise from the "new wave" of teachers, a wave in which you surf-rode when, in fact, you might have gone under or simply refused to get wet. It is well known that the first teacher determines a great deal of the handicapped child's future progress. How fortunate, then, you were. During your last week in the kindergarten, she drew the junior building in your homework book and, underneath, a poignant sketch of the children who were remaining with her: "Mandy sez bie-bie tω-everybody."

And now you have a special new book which, with its chic wallpaper cover, looks like a pamphlet of poems from a private press; but inside it has the new faces, one to a page, and the trunks and the arms and the legs, all in vivid colors. Here you are too, the tallest of the eight, your head a bunker of beribboned saffron supported by your elastic neck and those never-still legs. Your grin is giddy, which it always is when not diffidently gentle, and I suspect you have all the qualifications to become the class's clown. Already you have trespassed onto the high-school slide in an individualistic sortie that might have won you a broken neck; already, confronted with a student teacher in a trendy blouse and a crimson mini-skirt, you have shown your importunate passion for pretty clothes by leaping upon the girl and embracing her outfit, joyfully wetting yourself in the act.

Oo, you cry in the presence of what you find beautiful, *oo-oo!* "She is a girl," your new head teacher said of you, "with a mind of her own." Yes: the more we read your mind, the more we realize whose it is —not any of ours, not school's, not teacher's, not Karen's, Adrian's, Katrina's, Derek's, Lyn's, Mel's or Mike's, although like all of them in the baroque gallery in the homework book you clutch a red-and-yellow striped popsicle big as a ping-pong bat. Getting very sociable, you are; and yet—raw source of energy that you also are, given to using the bodies of others as mattresses or launching pads, and homing intimately in as you do on people's recent injuries and vulnerable parts—you remain just a bit the autist of the breakfast table, gifted with a knack for stark concentration, for looking into the essence of an umbrella or a bird cage, for outstaring brightest indirect sunlight. On the one hand, at the local library, on the same day as you impassively studied the little Thalidomide boy whose hands jutted from the fringes of his shoulders like fingered wings and walked on twelve-inch-square platforms of inch-thick wood for balance, you impulsively wheeled away the old man sitting reading in his wheelchair, thinking he needed a ride, I suppose, *un petit tour,* a bit of mothering, maybe. On the other hand, you sit in trances, interrupting yourself only to hoot *bye-bye!* and point violently away, which is where we should go. To pester you further is to incur what I these last few days have watched seachange and bloom: a putrid-looking bruise, the signature of an impersonally delivered karate-type punch—not to hurt anyone but to fend off irrelevance, to divide what you want from what you don't.

Captivated bafflement has therefore become our mode of life, caught as we are between your compulsive sociability, your animal high spirits, and your Garbo remotenesses, your Zen-disciplined immobility. And we guess a lot: play you (pardon the idiom) by ear. It's always something of a relief to find you doing something ordinary, something neither calisthenic nor separatist, something which doesn't reinforce what I call the Manda effect, which is a double phenomenon: numbed eardrums from the volume of your coloratura self-accompaniment while romping; and anticlimactic pinging when you desist, as if, like Pascal, we have discovered the silence of all space and feel frightened by it.

Boyd you now care for with enigmatic gentleness. You shout to him (in warning?) and then, with those powerful wiry arms, lift down his cage and set it centrally on the coffee table. It is high, so you stand on a chair to get it, as you do when ferreting after stogies to snap in half, nail varnish to tint your toenails with, a new toilet air freshener to sniff at. Yank down the wire door, thrust your arm into the cage in preliminary greeting, and then to work. Lift out the balsa-wood-light chunk of cuttlefish bone which is for calcium, then the spray of millet, while Boyd vaults and flutters in routine panic. Now the four dung-sullied perches and the ladder of white round rods. Slide out the tray with its sandpaper carpet, bear it gingerly to the back door of the house and tip on the grass the old grit, the spilled seed, and the accumulated bird lime. At once the sparrows come down on the debris like Assyrians. The sandpaper you leave where it falls and the tray you bring in after giving it a summary knock against the wall and, for good measure in the very act of walking back, bang it like a gong with your fist. Rinse in hot water and dry it with the special cloth. Lay Boyd's fresh floor (the sandpaper is limp, feels oily on the back) and slide the tray back in, giving it a slam if it sticks. Flap the millet against your wrist and set it back on the sandpaper. Over the waste basket, rub the cuttlefish bone with a handful of tissues and then reinstall while Boyd in the corner near his round red-rimmed mirror stares at himself with self-conscious nervousness. Next the abandonedly scattered sand and Tonic Grit (the makers claim it "acts as teeth to the bird" and "is free from any harmful decaying matter"). Flinging the stuff, you look like Marianne who sows on old French stamps: *la française,* but she, assuredly, would never try to make Boyd *eat* his sand or grit. A gay sprinkle across the room—we find it later in the toes of our shoes, in our hair, and sometimes in the butter, so mysteriously you make it travel—and you are done.

Lift out, always in this order, the pot of birdseed and the pot of water, which both clip behind the end bars, and march with the first to the back door again, there to puff off the husks while stirring the contents with a forefinger and squinting your eyes against the lifted chaff. Back in the kitchen, refill with Golden Life Birdseed, which is "superenriched with six extra ingredients including iodine, vitamins, and lysine, and ensures brighter cere—perfection of claw and beak—a longer, happier, healthy life." (G. L. Birdseed provides an advisory service too and we, I suppose, should provide Boyd with such extras as chickweed, watercress, and dandelion leaf.) Now slip the seed pot back and then the replenished water one. Boyd moves not at all during this (mostly, anyway).

All that remains it to wash-wipe the perches and the

ladder, replace them, which you do with much magenta-faced grunting while your hair tumbles and flows with your body's motion, and then, after a quick stroke along the crossbar of the non-removable wire swing, attend to Boyd's luxury item, the honey cone shaped like a bell and made of honey-coated seeds—which he prefers to seed that's plain, no matter how "Golden." Boyd is a gourmet.

Your finger curls now diagonally along one of the perches and Boyd stations himself with one claw on you, one on the wood, backing both chances: the perch's somehow foundering like the Bridge of San Luis Rey or, much likelier, your growing impatient with repose and launching him suddenly upward to flap and plunge about the cage, setting the tiny bell a-jingle while you pursue him with cupped hand. Soon he is caught, and, each time he is, I marvel at the rigid gentleness of your clasp, my mind on Lenny in Steinbeck's *Of Mice and Men*. But you know your own strength, even while squeeze-caressing the magical *livingness* of his groomed green body, and he doesn't fuss or wriggle. When you let him go, but only to slip the tip of a finger into his bird's armpit as he fans loose from you, you cackle-chirp mellowly and offer him a whole series of prods, pokes, and knuckle flicks, your fingers playing an invisible piccolo. *Fowler* is the word that occurs to me, except you pose no threat to him beyond the mussing of a few feathers, which he always corrects by a regal, miniature full stretch, wings taut and shivering, his chest fluffed out and one or two smoke puffs of moult drifting down to the grit and sand. Now he dips his head low and swings down deep from eleven o'clock through six to four, anti-clockwise, launching himself upside-down into the farthest corner while you, more and more excited, gesture as if to pound or pluck him, your stab at his tail feathers always a second late. Speeding up, you ringmaster him through his full repertoire of forward rolls and swift, thudding vaults, sometimes actually detaining him by his claws or a surprise finger hoop, but never too hard.

And I watch as you almost deliriously engage this other creature in sport while the afternoon light thins out: nothing of you is unengaged; no part of your mind holding back, spare and critical. You fly your sturdy hand inside his cage, pirouetting and bouncing with him in rumbustious awe, there being no verbal exchange with him and no second chance once he is damaged. It's the same you as does cartwheels and somersaults on the grass, as if movement were everything and meditation naught. You meet him on a level of impulse and reflex where not many humans belong; and, sometimes, when acute jubilation pulls other feelings and cravings from deep within you, I see your fun bloat just a little with the urge to see just how much more this animated, inaudible puppet can stand. You brim with a voluptuous power that could pulp him in five seconds (your grip on any non-hairy wrist leaves bruises), and you very nearly begin the silken arctic shiver of making yourself irremediably felt; of maiming without being hurt and without sharing his pain. But no, you mercilessly fell vases and pictures when the mood takes you, and big humans too; Boyd you affably torment in what looks like a baby *corrida,* and all you want to do (so to speak) is plant a rosette between his horns, give some other being a run that sets you both a-tremble, and then suck on a big ice cream. Sometimes you stir your arm in the cage as if mixing a cake, and I half-think exuberance is moving today into battery and butchery; but I no longer offer to curb you, having learned that you uncannily restrain yourself. Slight birds are not children, and you know, and even if you squashed the chirp out of them at a rate of one a week, I'd still keep you in birds in the belief that one day you'd come to handle life gently just from feeling it time and again buck and twist and throb in your fist. Which you seemed to learn the first time you slid your arm into the cage: *caramba! dig that green-and-yellow bird but don't dig him no grave.*

Only the other day (you're tough on *you*) you picked up a brand-new pencil sharpener, plugged your forefinger into the larger of the two holes and began to sharpen it, wincing hardly at all as the blade sank in, or, later as you held your pouring finger in the stream from the cold-water tap. Never what could be called a crybaby, you live by an unvoiced, hardly even acknowledged code which says the injured press on regardless; all that is permitted is an extravagant, half-amused bellow at the indignity suffered, to be followed by a complete change in activity. Somehow you know you have been enigmatically hurt, not by anything so minor as pencil sharpeners, but by chemistry; hurt even before beginning, and this knowledge informs your conduct with all creatures. An antagonistic and often histrionic compassion is your life style, as if you think we are all hurt and, although you're willing to salute the fact in a civil and sensitive way, loathe all vulnerability. I think you have assumed that Boyd is hurt; otherwise he wouldn't be in a cage at all (just as we wouldn't be in a house). And for your chagrined expostulations I think we should reward you as best we can—reward you, I mean, with something that your mind finally decided to accost in bulk: birds.

Give yourself, since this is your secret favorite, the eagle, whom you try to outstare in all the zoos: a bird of bad moral character, according to Benjamin Franklin ("generally poor," he said, "and often very lousy"); a bird that relishes a tasty carcass—"And like a thunderbolt he falls"—although, for staring hard into the sun, he has been called stoical. He is best killed, as Aesop notes, with an arrow guided by flights made of eagle plumes. But—not to limit you or pander to you too much—also these, from me to you in one long chirrup: Poe's obstinate raven; Edward Lear's owl at sea in a pea-green boat with a cat; Long John Silver's parrot, Cap'n Flint, who said "Pieces of Eight" without pause or change, like the clacking of a tiny mill (which you would never hear, I'm afraid); the jackdaw of Rheims; the dodo, the kiwi, the phoenix of Arabia; four and twenty blackbirds encased in pastry; the nightingales that sang for apeneck Sweeney; the wild swans at Coole that "scatter, wheeling" with a positive bell-beat of wings; the albatross which came through the snow-fog and, although a bird of good omen, was inhospitably killed by a cantankerous ancient mariner almost as old as Thomas Hardy's darkling thrush, "frail, gaunt, and small"; John Hall Wheelock's fish hawk fanning heavily over the sea in "crumbling light"; Gerard Manley Hopkins' skylark with its "rash-fresh re-winded new-skeined score/In crisps of curl off wild winch whirl"; the magical, delicate firebird of Stravinsky; the golden cockerel of Rimsky-Korsakov; the twenty-four birds of Aristophanes who speak in short-syllabled chorus and whose arrival on stage is usually omitted from *The Birds,* but whose noise evokes a Hitchcock film:

EUELPIDES: How they thicken, how they muster,
             How they clutter, how they cluster.
             Now they scramble here and there,
             Now they scramble altogether.
             What a fidgeting and clattering!
             What a twittering and chattering,
             Don't they mean to threaten us? What think you?
PISTHETAIROS: Yes, I think they do.

(Will you one day get your tongue round those? Euelpides, Pisthetairos, Euelpisthet— *eel*—pidesairos!) And the squeaking, cheeping, shrilly whinnying, bazooka-yodeling pop-the-weasel popping of Respighi's own private parliament of musical fowls and two corbies from an old Scottish song and Walt Whitman's two sea birds courting on the shore and the bird Picasso's chauffeur found dead in the street and which Picasso painted into life again on a branch of blossom in 1939 and the sociable, blanched doves which nested on his balcony when he was painting variations on Velázquez' *"Las Meninas"* and the Little Owl, rough-cast and armored in painted bronze, Picasso again of course, and, and

of Chagall, a salmon-bright tumbling rooster elongated, a beaked juggler in red and green and yellow and with Uncle Neuch the fiddler leaning against his ribs from where he stands inside the bird, and one sumptuous enameled cock riding the night sky like a stallion,

as well as (*puff-puff!*) larks, nightingales, cuckoos, robins, supplied retail by John Keats and William Wordsworth and Percy Bysshe Shelley and Robert Bridges and Vachel Lindsay, windhovering all of them; hurt hawks by Robinson Jeffers, one Ibsenian wild duck from Norway, one fancy bluebird from Belgium, dirge singers transformed into birds by Nature's ordinance and François Rabelais (clerijays, bishojays, gormanders and one popinjay), penguins by Anatole France, harpies whom the Aztecs called winged wolves, and mucky-rumped Stymphalides, together with one nest thief out of Brueghel (he who knows where the nest is, knows it; he who takes it, owns it—except the peasant in the foreground is pointing at the climbing boy with derisive permissiveness and is himself the fool, walking straight into a pond!), an owl and a nightingale, a disputatious pair out of the Middle Ages, Icarus who flew so near the sun the wax in his ears melted, a frigate bird which eats flying fish, a flamingo from the famous colony in the Camargue where the white horses and the wild bulls are, an oystercatcher called Sea-Pie (white and black pied), a rook which builds high and so junks the adage of fine summers when rooks build high, a shrike which professionally impales its kill, a goldcrest, small enough to fit into a pingpong ball if you let the tail protrude

and so to earth, where, as if mummified, you are staring through Boyd like Picasso's violet woman examining her blackened mirror, lost in a cage where every day is approximately silent, and ignorant of this bird hoard I bring you: gifts as well-meant and irrelevant, maybe, as the food, flowers, photographs, paintings, cowbells, shotguns, and puppies, parrots, national costumes, boxes of money and cars (including a Lincoln convertible sedan) that pour in to Picasso's villa. He welcomes, we hear, the national costumes and puts them on: a Yugoslav robe, an African cap, and so would you, agreeably wearing whatever plumage we devise for you, and reckoning the wide world your benefactor.

I'd better finish soon, before you hit the house from school. *The East,* we say, *will soon be here,* as if half the globe were going to descend upon us as incubus. Yet nothing seems real until you are back.

Here, to play with, is that old chestnut of ours, the original Japanese hieroglyph for bird:

becoming, through abstraction, the modern character drawn thus:

Some bird! A bird box, rather, or a bird cage, on a single sled runner. Japanese has almost two thousand of these "characters" whereas European languages use a Roman script of only twenty-six letters. Yet, I read (what I know already from observing you in the Babel-laboratory of your own near-language), Roman is confusing: *a* looks like *o* and *u* like *v*, and *b* mirrors *d*, *p* mirrors *q*. And how do you pronounce such a deduced-from-practice orthographical freak as *ghieti*, meaning "fish," the *gh* coming from *laugh*, the *ie* from *anomalies*, and *ti* from *contradiction*? Lucky the Japanese children, especially those of them who, as you sometimes do, mirror write; bird remains bird, although flying in the opposite direction, whereas *dub* isn't *bud* any more than *pal* is *lap*. What a pity we can't backtrack you through the history of signs to the Ancient Egyptian bovine head which eventually became *A*, the cross stroke being vestigial horns; and then bring you forward in time to *A*.

Or so I inappropriately think, for what has *A* to do with a bull's head? Why bother discovering why *A* is the shape it is? No, *A* is *A*, having an abstract life of its own, and surely we have lost, having to add *ull* to *b* or *ow* to *c* or *x* to *o*, referring to instead of recognizing ☙ (or, as it is in Sinai script, ⚹, like one of those sun-whitened horned steer skulls you see in the badlands in Westerns; picked clean, which our spellings are not). Maybe, in these hairy-eyeball times, we are too visual by far: "Ripeness is all" will soon be given a redundant visual translation on TV (commercial for corn?); but I can't help thinking four to five years is the wrong age to be substituting abstraction for observation. When a Japanese adult draws the character for "bird" he draws a quasi-picture of what he can see daily in his garden, outside his office window, whereas *bird* takes us beyond *brid*, in Old English, only as far as our old friend, Etym. Dub. And

Etym. Dub. isn't a bird at all, any more than *A* is a cow's head or a bird's visual impression of a cow's head is anything but part of his word for a cow's head. But if you only part master the alphabet, I promise to shut up. It's all a matter of point of view. Charlie Greene, the American sprinter, was asked why he wore sunglasses to race in. Not sunglasses, he answered: *these are my reentry shields*. Point of view, indeed, like that reentry technique called lipreading. *It rate ferry aren't hadn't four that reason high knit donned co*—which, as Alexander Graham Bell revealed, is how the lipreader sees *It rained very hard and for that reason I did not go* It all depends on how you look at things: glad over Kierkegaard's 70,000 fathoms; glad all the same.

4.

Babel 100 Plus

Let us now make personal history and unlock your word hoard, not only to celebrate it but to make sure we understand each other as best we can. Some of the words are unorthodox things, to be sure, and like items from some extra-galactic code remain a little out of reach, identifiable certainly but hard to explain. From time to time you invent a new one, although not as often as you pick up a new word that is orthodox. Sometimes you gain a word only to discard one (from your everyday speech at any rate), so it's no wonder that our tiny lexicon is always out of date, not quite representative and studded with optimistic guesses. That's, of course, the serious view of words and you (Words-and-You), whereas we usually find ourselves in a state of beaming jubilation with every word you seem to acquire or understand—even when, as quite often, we are mistaken and have too eagerly interpreted something you uttered that wasn't a word at all!

But, mistaken or not, we find ourselves wanting to grab— what? oh—this imported package, say, of thin Swiss *Chocolat Suchard au lait avec raisins macérés au Cointreau,* and give you all, and to hell with the injunction on the wrapper, *ne doit pas être remis aux enfants.* It's adult chocolate, you see, like Lowenbrau is grownup beer and *dyslexic* is a grownup word you might never need. Never mind, you aren't the world's most conspicuous consumer of chocolate anyway, whether it's Cointreau-potent or not, and I'm no Cointreau addict, ever since on the *Mauretania,* long before you were born, sailing westward to New York, in catastrophic weather of the kind that looks thrilling when painted in oils, they kept serving orange ice cream to those who showed up in the dining room. . . .

Now to my list of mingled code and right speech, penciled here before me on one biscuit-colored sheet like independence being declared. What was it that Borges, the almost-blind Argentinian writer, said while he was signing the copies of his books in the Rare Book Room one term last year? *Word mad,* he told us in his excellent British English, "I am word mad!" At that time, *blanc,* meaning white but sounding so close to black, was the particular word exercising him; and the point being made by a man who couldn't really see us as he talked gained especial force.

Exercising (indeed, distinctly irritating) me as I write this on a sodden autumn morning, there's this blanched L.P. downgraded to cardboard—a color disc, sitting on the desk, with 298 Spectroliac shades fanning out from the center on both sides with a selector that isolates any one fourteen-degree segment from the others so you can see the color better. Except that none of the colors have names; only numbers, so that what I'm sure is duck-egg blue is 504 or 506 and what I call chimpanzee's-anus pink (color of my office walls!) is merely 330. One day you might get around to learning "Richard Of York Gave Battle In Vain" for remembering the spectrum in its right order: red, orange, yellow, green, blue, indigo, violet. I found it useful myself when working just recently on a novel based on the spectrum, but I like it fine in its own right too, a spectral mnemonic that's every bit as much fun as Newton's hapless old apple must have been to him, considering he'd also figured out the innards of white light as well. But this dreary color disc, it's like a standing reproof to all word men, turning you through the spectrum to the tune of 0-006†, 2009††, 1008††, and so on. Why, I read, on the center of the disc where it should supply the title and group and composer, "Insist on Spectroliac BRILLIANT SUPER WHITE. It's the the *blackest* white paint you can buy." Why not instead, the *blackest* white paint (Borgesiac) you can't buy but have to wheedle out of Isaac Newton by quoting his *Principia* to him entire, Let's get back to our *moutons* (mot-ons?); woids after boids.

In the beginning are these words.

appul (apple): no doubt about this, you fetch them off the tree yourself. First you munch the flesh, then lick the knifed-off peels as if they're the fins of some elegant, recently discovered fish, your tongue relishing the curvature rather than the taste. I'm not sure; but I do know that the pupil, once supposed to be a solid body, is the apple of the eye. This fruit is supposed to be forbidden. Juno, Minerva, and Venus competed for the golden apple of discord that rewards beauty; now, if only *you*'d been there. . . . The Dead Sea apple turns to ashes. Did you know apple butter was a sauce or preserve made from apples stewed in cider? Apples repel doctors and applejohns have shriveled jackets. I keep looking at this word—APPLE—and suddenly it becomes unfamiliar: mere letters that correspond to nothing I know, and I begin to know how you feel when confronted with a long word in print.

Aroo (Andrew), who was in the same kindergarten class as you and whom you, in your vague and luxurious way, find in your new class although he isn't there at all. Maybe you see his face where he might yet appear, where he is destined to be; I'll believe that, or that he's your *Doppelgänger,* the boy who (wasn't it Andrew?) accidentally locked himself in the toilet at your birthday party and accordingly lost his chunk of cake to the madding crowd.

That ends the *a*'s I'm afraid, but the next letter is a favorite with you, for which fact there are famous phonological reasons. *Bababab*a, you used to cry; well, the southern Ancient Greeks called the northern ones "barbarians" for speaking an uncouth idiom that sounded like *bar-bar* without variation. Ba-ba, black-sheep Greeks they were.

bar (bath): the contemplation of which, even when it's empty, soothes you almost as much as cavorting in one that is full. Candidates for the order of knighthood called the Bath used to bathe formally before installation. It is not anywhere said *if* they were ever obliged or permitted to bathe again. I hereby constitute you a candidate.

Be (Beard) is Santa Claus symbolized by his beard, but has, as yet, nothing to do with what grows on my own chin, or with the beak bristles of birds. But we'll keep trying.

beebee (drink) is a noun verging on being a verb as well; one of those words you have invented (probably from "tea"). It summons up for you the intricate rituals of bedtime and breakfast, the potion always being tea or a milky drink almost viscous with cornflour. Usually, when saying it, you raise an imaginary cup toward your mouth or, if impatient, make an upward flick with cupped hand. Perhaps, though, you subliminally know some Latin and allow yourself this word out of *bibere* (to drink), which gave us *bibbing* and *bibulous*. Or I am wrong and this is the cloth square strung under a baby's chin with tapes: the *bib,* the blotter that takes the slips between cup and lip. Or it is the whiting-pout, a fish with an inflatable membrane over its eyes; or the Aryan verb *bhi* (*-bhi*), meaning to quiver, or the Persian *bibi,* meaning a lawful wife, or even William Beebe, explorer of the Galápagos Islands!

bir (beer) is a surreptitious, fleeting word which you resort to only on special occasions when you think you'll get your own way; an opportunistic monosyllable, therefore, pleading on an ascending scale for a sip of mine, a spoonful dropped into your glass of lemonade, an emptied beer can refilled with lemonade (akin to whiskey's being put into old sherry casks, except you let nothing mature) or, such is the word's scope, a tiny bottle of imitation champagne. When you steal beer, you do that in mercenary silence, breathing too hard with stealth and effort to address even yourself; feigning, maybe, that what you don't verbalize you aren't guilty of. And, when you do say *bir,* you expect our delight at your having used a word to override our disapproval of your request. I hereby award you a suet halo for ingenuity.

blun (balloon) we in its incalculably plural form blow up until we look like those apple-cheeked faces on old maps—Boreas, Australis, etc.—with feedback inflating our jowls. Or like Goya's boy inflating a bladder, Goya who lived in "The House of the Deaf Man." *Bluns* come in all shapes, sizes, colors, but mostly long-sausage, twelve-inch, and blue or yellow, and some *bluns* even have tiny inflatable horns on the inflatable heads of demons, dragons, or super-germs, which to my mind is a triumph of what some manufacturers with untentional wit call "preshaped conture." Whatever variety we bought, we always did the same with them: filled them with water and other fluids and lodged them, distended and ungainly, in the seats of cinemas. (My generation of kids, I mean, a long time back.) *Bluns* you hang on all door handles in a perpetual pneumatic Christmas which, for some reason private to you, exempts them all from the flashing spikes of your brandished umbrellas. Which is just as well for of the bang of a balloon punctured you are dead afraid. That sound, or the bang of a paper bag blown up and burst, is the crack of childhood doom for you, whether you're wearing your hearing aids or not. (This is why, in the humid days of summer, overventilated friends should not succor themselves in your presence by blowing into doggy bags or supermarket jumbo sizes; you anticipate the bang and flee.) At a school party, a game played with balloons held between the legs put you almost over the brink. But, in its proper place and proper condition (kidney-firm, nozzle doubled over and choked off with a double thread, as well as absolutely stationary), the *blun* has your unquestioning loyalty, holds you in thrall. We have, at the moment, about two dozen suspended around the house, but not always in the same places on successive days; the *bluns* in fact circulate according to a program only you possess (a bit like those Mexican Olympics). So to move around at night without thorough lighting is to have an occasional rubbery paunch of a Lilliputian brushing the face or the back of a hand. Boyd, I hope, will never set his claws on one of them; and may the hot tips of our cigarettes always miss them, and all mirrors, windows, light bulbs and frangible Christmas-tree baubles keep their splinters to themselves and pins into their cushions sink more deeply and writer's needle-sharp 2B pencils point only where they should, rose stems be scabbarded, rough jewelry be abraded smooth, filed nails with tips like spear grass be scythed down blunt, and all careless handlers be exiled by Montgolfier hot-air *blun* to the Republican convention that released the most balloons from the nets near the ceiling. Even so, what with doors being still in use in this house, and the rate of rubber rot being what it is, one or another element in your gaudy balloon barrage is bound to be blowing up soon, just as others, without so much as a sigh or a thread-thin hiss, shrink down into leprous-looking oblate spheroids (especially those you have painted faces upon in mud-thick poster-colors). No one remembers a fallen balloon, not even if, like each of yours, it's had a word blown into it along with good old, bad old, human gas. But, one day, throw balloons you will, big bangs or not.

And so to *bo* (escalator), a word we've already rejoiced about in this space probe of an epistle that makes me sometimes feel like one of those men Herman Melville had in mind when he said, "I love all men that *dive* . . . the whole corps of intellectual thought-divers that have been diving & coming up again with bloodshot eyes since the world began." Very much bloodshot these pearls get from peering at my own scribble. Anyway, Saturday mornings, up you glide on successive escalators to the sixth floor of the same department store, toys on the ground floor, toilet at the top. You ride with sublime abstractedness and have developed a lovely, demure off-step by means of which you find yourself walking a fraction of a second before your feet touch down. *Blasée,* I'd call you, escalating as you do in the old sense of that overworked and underachieving word, *escalading*—an even older word—by storming fortified places by means of scaling ladders and emitting at shrewdly chosen intervals your war cry of an unappeased Hottentot (which announces there is something at the top of the *bo* you always expect but never find)—the Palladium, Greek version? the statue of Pallas, the ancient Dewline on which the safety of Troy depended? Or just a Houston Astrodome-sized lollipop with strobe lights whipping around inside? Give us time and we'll lay one on:

O/C Pipe Dreams to O/C Equipment: Troy. REQUISITION AT ALL COSTS SITUATION ESCALATING AM CONTAINING REBEL FORCE WITH HASTILY IMPROVISED CARDBOARD MOCK-UPS BUT THESE NON-MOVING KINDLY CABLE CARS AND COGS IMPERATIVE YOU STRIP AIRPORTS RAILWAY TERMINALS IF NECESSARY ALSO CHECK DESIGN DESIGNER FIRST BO ALMOST CERTAINLY USA CIRCA 1900 NO DOUBT PATENTED CAN WE BRIBE SOMEBODY URGENTLY REQUIRE BEAU GESTE.

Seemingly cognate, but not, *boa!* is an exuberant plea for us to tickle you, preferably while rolling with you on bed or floor. The game begins with the tickler-to-be tightening his lips as if holding in his breath with some difficulty and then requires a rapid succession of b-b-b-b-b which consummates itself in an explosive shout of *boa!* as the tickle suddenly begins. A joy word of your own devising, it's very recent and dionysian whereas *bo* is old and is an Apollonian affirmative that you utter while upraising a stiff *heil*ing arm whose index finger points at the top floor of an invisible six-floor department store. *Bo* can be said to a goose, like *boo* or *boh,* or to other children when you play Bo-Peep and erupt from your hiding place. *Boa,* though, you can't say except to a Brazilian snake or an Old World python, both of which will attempt to get you round the neck, which is not only why a certain kind of tippet is called a feather boa but why, perhaps, your invitation to the constrictions of tickle-tumble comes out a bit strangulated, every bit a tapering diphthong expressive of British English at its *moewst refaeined* but also of speech in certain parts of Pennsylvania where (perhaps) something was left over from the wars. A sound like a cone, the "bo" of *bo* and *boa,* comes into being, I know not why, out of the rain forests of British class-consciousness, out of the dark satanic fallout of industrial Pennsylvania, and might just as well in its constricted, garroted way come out of the depths of Brazil where, as John Donne tells us in a phrase of hyperbolical precision, *the sun dines,* and where you can only get around by

boat, the word, which, as we've said, meant "water" until you got *worbar* and now figures only in the Botany Bay of your vocabulary where even the sun cannot reach, a boat not being an object you think worth referring to (not often, anyway), much as you love sailing and steaming vessels both great and small.

Prompted and prodded, you'll say *boat* and mean boat; but somehow, girl, you separated *boat* from *worbar* without getting boats, almost as if boats that float are conceptually submerged, and therefore *worbar* includes all boats and maybe even all who sail in them. To say *worbar* is, virtually, to be a shipowner supreme, which you already are in physical miniature (although, fair's fair, you run just as big an airport as you do a dockyard). You'll come back to this word one day, but only, I believe, if you never board a hydrofoil again and so never again develop that morgue face quite unlike the children's faces in the sailing bits of Claude Lelouch's lyrically colored family movie, *A Man and a Woman*. Only at the very edge is the sea your friend, and its many-voicedness is wasted anyway on you; and only on the fringes of your mind are there verbal boats, whose noblest function is to float the soap for you at bathtime. "Ship," of course, which would refine your vessel sense, you relentlessly ignore, no matter how many Cunarders I show you.

Bobbee (Bobby) is another of those kindergarten friends whose faces have vanished while their names remain; these cannot, by any stretch of imagination, be replaced, whereas something can always be managed with your friends who have feathers, all Boyds being

boid and a good many *boids* capable of being Boyd. Although, recently, you have begun to say this sometimes as *burr,* you long ago entangled it with *boy,* so that sometimes you seem to see the boys in school with a fowler's eye and sometimes Boyd as a candidate for junior school. The difference, though, is that Boyd frightens you not at all (you make him serve you), whereas the boys in kindergarten perturbed you keenly at first, being rougher than anything you'd met and outnumbering you two girls three to one. So you took it out on me, the biggest approximately submissive boy you could find; but not so often now—somewhere along the line, I think, you applied muscle and bone to your tormentors, and that would be a memorable experience for them. Boys have also—meek as Boyd himself— succumbed to your disdainful receptivity, recognizing in you a force old as Bathsheba, and especially the svelte little Pakistani, who gives you a pat and a furtive hug when he thinks the others boys aren't looking. Names don't matter, but these gestures to one another out of your respective overpowering privacies are like mountains moving.

boo (bosom) you'll use only when reciting, with enumerative zeal, the list of your facial and bodily parts. I've heard you, seen you, sitting alone at a larger mirror and pronouncing them with finicking precision while observing the shapes your lips make as they move. This physiognomical-anatomical cantata never included *chest,* a word you don't get because it begins with a sound you can't hear or see. Lucky for you, then, you're a girl; boys, having no bosom, have simply no chests at all.

brow, which you enunciate immaculately, belongs in the same list as *boo,* and only repeated insistences will make you say it on its own. You seem to disdain the conflicts, the rough-and-tumble, the mix-up, of language, preferring words in congruent groups or words in isolation to any combination in which there's contrast and clash, genre against genre or even noun against verb; after all, a verb gets a noun into motion, a motion that might never end until the noun's disappeared forever. Single words, like single slides and single umbrellas, appear to be inexhaustible objects of contemplation, and to combine them—especially on the conceptual level—is perhaps to modify them irreparably. Eyebrow pencil on the eyebrow (*brow* is always *eye*-brow to you) is one thing; indeed, a favorite sport of yours. But *eye* plus *brow* you spontaneously mistrust and won't say, intent on the independence of the one vis-à-vis the other. Such is your Zen; you gaze, or so I conjecture, at the form and the atoms, seeing all as a chip off the aboriginal cosmic working block, paying homage to a uniqueness which syntax, metaphor, and connotation actually spoil. And when you stop looking, you have probably assimilated the object—as it is in this time and this place—*into you* more thoroughly than any of us assimilate the lessons we claim to learn.

No generalist, you have something in common with the Eskimos, who have several different words for snow according to its condition and kind. You haven't the words, but I think you'd note the differences between different snows: the wet, the crumbly, the caked, the packed, the snow that will not last and the snow that has come to stay. The Swedes use different words for when, say, you *go* in a train, when a train *goes*, when a pilot *goes* up in his plane, and when you *go* across the road. On the one hand, you are Swedish (which by blood you partly are anyway) and Eskimo in attentiveness; on the other, though, your handicap prevents you from attaining even to the superficialities of English. Your no doubt exquisite perceptions just cannot be said (and I realize and defy the hazards of articulating them for you).

On the one hand again, the economy of Basic English's sixteen verbs only is just right for you, but, on the other, you are the very person to multiply the the modes of all the verbs there are until they register nothing to anyone else. Those Eskimo variants of snow are communal property, whereas you, for all your behavioral rigidity, know that the pencil *meets* the eyebrow differently on each penciling occasion and that *meet* (or *apply,* say) disregards what is unique to each. The categorical, I gather from your intent frowns and your long, long scrutinies, would always be too crude for you, yet that is the very thing you need to get started at all.

If we fantasize, we can elaborate the verb *to pencil* into *browpencil* and so on until we get *browapencili* (for when a sharp pencil touches a ruffled eyebrow), *browopencilu* (for when a blunt pencil touches an unruffled eyebrow), *browopencilipo* (for when that happens briefly), *browopencilopi* (for when the contact is longer), and onward until micro-differences have bloated idiom to the point of paralysis. To live competently in the world, I conclude, entails a certain insensitivity—and a deliberate one too; otherwise, everything would fascinate us so much that we would lapse into highly attuned trances. The world, ironically enough, is here to be in part ignored, and whatever (in the jargon of the day) is mind-expanding militates against living successfully by orthodox standards.

Clearly (or at least shiningly through a dark prejudice), in order to have any chance at all of fending for yourself in the ordinary world, the supersensitivity which I infer from the intensity of your scrutinies must be chopped on the block of a primary vocabulary. And the same is true even if I'm wrong and, instead of being supersensitive, you spend much of your time in an inaccessible, ineffable blank. Either way, you will be deprived—I mean in the condition of being deprived—either of your supersensitivity (unless you regain it after humdrum years of learning how to buy bread, stamps, and shoes) or of the peace the blank brings with it. But I think it would be just as hard to get back to fine attunement through increasing articulateness between twelve and twenty as to achieve that attunement for the first time after being blank for so long. I just don't know; which doesn't mean I *almost* know: it means I've no idea at all, you're that inscrutable. So I'm wishing you the best, you the would-be cosmonaut who's never allowed out alone; I'm presuming you're a mystic rather than a non-starter, a simple soul rather than a cipher. Your privacy, I hope, is full, not empty.

brella, coming in slightly wrong alphabetical order (but let it stand because it exemplifies the wackiness you create around you), you say with ebullient relish provided that, before it or with it held in hand, you aren't singing a fully choreographed mantra. I won't, just here, go into your *brella* rituals; in fact we've touched on these already. What I've concluded is that umbrellas obsess you because they are two-in-one and therefore, to you who love uniqueness, represent magic. Up never interferes with down and vice versa. The two extremes are compatible and permit you a double view of a single thing, a single apprehension of a double possibility. When the *brella*'s up, you're overjoyed by its capacity for coming down, and when it's rolled and fastened you're overjoyed by what it's just been, what it can again be after a couple of simple shoves. The *as is* and the *can be* you rejoice in simultaneously, so much so that your conception of umbrella is mobile, not static (although, I suppose, a pretty static sort of mobility; pretty limited). *Brella* is big and therefore exercises a greater pull on you than such other adjustable items as knives, carving forks and sugar tongs. Only lamps and scissors have comparable magic. Parachutes, by the way, let you down in one half of their performance since they don't even retract, and a neatly folded parachute, at least as far as looks go, amounts to nothing at all.

bu is your truncation of omnibus, which you most love when it sways and almost pitches you from one side to the other. Then you laugh way up high. A mere smile you reserve for moments when familiar landmarks trail into view; and when they don't—if the route's been changed to avoid road constructions or if you're going to a new place—you show concern or alarm by an imperious frown or a nagging, interrogative wail. But buses please mostly and you draw them with heavy-handed joy.

bye-bye you have just begun to say, with ironic intonation and many hand movements, almost as if you believe no one will believe you mean it. But you do mean it, you do go, you do go to sleep, and you know this word is never final. But it is the last of your *b*'s, and leaving *b* behind to move on is like leaving the coast of California in order to visit the Pacific islands. Yet even a sandcastle built on an island beach makes you a landed proprietor in this dimension.

car you intone lengthily, confident that you know what you're about; and, sometimes, in impatience, you exclaim repeatedly with elaborate, unfurling motions of your arms, "no *car;* car *no!*" Which I reckon eloquent and am thankful for two words combined almost against your will.

cig, for cigarette, doesn't come readily to you; but if we point at one you'll name it with a smirk of sinful complicity. Maybe you know what most people don't who call on the weed: the word *could* have come from *cigarra,* which is Spanish for cicada. So—so, sing:

Have a cicada
Down on the old hacienda
Where never is coughed
A discouraging puff
And all our butt-ends-a
Sing nightly cadenzas.
Cough, cough, cough,
Huff, puff, huff.
It's still the magic wand that conjures up tomorrow's potable gold,
It's still lone man's companion, bachelor's friend, it's even called
Sublime.

You always roll your own, don't you? Or, taking up one of ours, touch the filter to your lips once with eye-squinting aplomb and set it back to do its worst to somebody else.

(About *chin*, now, a message to ourselves: see under *tsin*, as the guidebooks say. And look for *clock* under *lock*. All that kind of elbow nudging.)

dayn (ten) you can count up to at speed; in fact, you utter your numbers so fast that this one becomes something like *dey;* and *doo, dree* you hardly voice at all. You have a mischievous habit of regarding numbers as things to chant and not to use, just as, when counting on your fingers while chanting, you flash them erect in a succession almost too swift to follow. Yet when you first learned to count you sang out the numbers with triumphant resonance, your whole face alive with the emphasis. You like to identify things in twos and threes, but higher numbers interest you not at all —not for any practical purposes anyway. Maybe this is another sign of your disinclination to group things which, even if identical, you prefer to contemplate one by one. Your world is full of nomadic monads.

ding (swing) has no *an sich* to follow it; here you soar, no word to the person pushing you from behind, but, for his express guidance when you want more height, your index finger extends up the chain in mild, discreet imperative. The pusher soon learns to heed that sign; if he doesn't instantly work you back to horizontal on the forward lunge, you wheel round, booming like a bittern, your arm rigid and aimed at the sky while your cry pumps out and your finger stabs until you have been obeyed. Overhead the twin, triple, and quadruple jets skim or lumber over, low for you to view, and, ever in good humor toward them, you cant your head as if at the beginning of a parabola that takes you up to their silver bellies and over their uncluttered backs. Then the back swing that reinvigorates your climb and also, if the pusher be unlucky, clips him on the chin as he crouches to receive you. *Ding* it

Words for a Deaf Daughter   95

almost always is; but you have, after mustering your skills and calming your mouth muscles for a good five seconds, said the real thing: *z-z wi ngh!* A few times, with that *eureka* smirk. A phonetic golden egg.

dog (sometimes *dog-woof*), the last *d* I can think of, is a word you show no overpowering desire to use, but you understand it when we say it to you. Of the ritual dogs attending your bedtimes, more later; sufficient that they are of Hong Kong celluloid and will not thirst while waiting.

Under *e* we have *eye,* which you say well, *eigh* for "eight" and *ee!,* your call sign which you have finally civilized into a muted form that can be charming. *E-oe,* a fugitive from the *h*'s, is "hello," with which you bombard the telephone mouthpiece and greet the most pressing of your friends—those who demand of you *a word. E-even* is between ten and twelve but sometimes turns up between six and eight: a number strictly for vocal rendering in your descant of numbers, it signifies nothing as yet. But about *ellow* you are utterly certain, it being one of your favorite colors.

file, the tool, is a recent word that you say beautifully with patience, poise, and a craftsman's graveness; and *fur,* as found on the inside of your new white boots, is something you caress your cheek against and also find on Boyd's belly, most gollys' heads. And *g* is for *gawyee,* alias not only golliwog but also any Negro. Sitting in a train one day and studying the human pageant through the plate-glass window with the air of Queen Victoria having to inspect a tear bottle full of Lord Alfred Tennyson's dandruff, you shivered with astonishment when a colored porter wheeled something past: a live golly, whom you at once extolled with a hysterical shout and whom, no doubt, you'd love to hang on your long line until the Scotch tape dried out and he fell behind the sofa. What you think your Pakistani friend actually is, or what you sometimes might even call him (he has a thick mat of curly hair), I'd rather think I needn't guess. Nonsense words have nonsensical consequences. Finally, here, *gibig,* for guinea pig, one of which your class had in kindergarten. Sometimes, for a joke (which, in you, is highly sophisticated word play), you point to yourself and tell us you're a *gibig,* and we have to contradict you with tops-of-our-voices vehemence. It's a reassuring game.

fy means "fire," but also the cuttingness of knives and the lion sun captured in some mustards. You also, when in peak declamatory mood, say it as *var,* like a long-frozen Viking pitching a war cry through whiskers still congealed, so fusing enthusiastic awe with a finger-wagging parody of all wise adults. It is also your word for portable electric heaters, and at these—if they have convection vanes rotating under a mock-coal carapace full of roseate light—you'll stare a full hour, enraptured by the glow and cozy flicker of the non-coals. You know it isn't coal; you saw me touch it once and you couldn't understand why no blister came. Prudent, you still won't touch, though. One metamorphosis brings others with it, and perhaps you think the real and fake coal alternate and half the coal touchers get burned. A burning match, though, you will puff out, letting the breath as it comes out make an accidental word that sounds like *pun.*

The *h* you refuse to "hello" you paradoxically give to *hawz* (horse), having ridden on an Exmoor pony, *har* (hair) and *hot-oo!* (to be exclaimed in the presence of fires, mustards, knives, etc.). But "hammer" you also deprive of its aspirate, your preference being to call it *pomper,* whether it's one of your plastic lightweights or the real iron one with a claw head. Wielded heftily enough—so your philosophy of percussion goes—a *pomper* will right anything: umbrellas, books, chair covers, bleeding fingers, recalcitrant Boyd, and even broken windows or wine glasses.

Bash a thing hard enough and it will repair itself. Always, with those big dry-palmed hands of yours, striated as if you were fifty, you try the *pomper* remedy before anything else. You have a lovely swing but hardly any aim, hence the hammer can never quite keep pace with the damage it does while mending.

ie-gree we supply to you almost wholesale in cones, wafers, and (when you're obviously in a gargantuan mood) bricks. As often as not, though, ice cream alone isn't enough for you, and you'll dip a popsicle or a lollipop into the thick of it, then use either of these as a spatula to paint us with or (in quieter mood) as a tasting tool. You prefer both hands busy, there being about you something of the artisan, which we find some consolation when daubed with an ice-cream impasto only seconds after you irrupt into the house from school. Down slams the door of the freezer compartment and you haul out the day's frozen booty, hedonist, action painter and bandit in one. You once tried to cement cracks in the walls with this commodity, like a snow queen turned laborer, but soon discovered the facts of thawing and did not persist. Had there been no Bonnie for Clyde, you would have made a high-class stand-in.

No *j*'s yet, and there wouldn't be a *k* if we didn't habitually think of "school" as *kool*. You say this with a little wavy writing motion of your hand; you plead for *kool* endlessly, and you check each morning with us to ascertain if today is *kool, bo* or *ding*. Or, rather, you used to; nowadays you seem to place and identify the days rather well, not knowing their names yet, but capably locating painting day (Wednesday) as the one before swimming day, which comes before come-home-early day, Friday; after which it's plain sailing (if you can be said to do anything plain or plainly) through Saturday and Sunday (*bo* day and *ding*-in-park day respectively). Only the early part of the week puzzles you, especially Tuesday, a limbo occasion whose only definition so far is its being in between. But the breakthrough will come soon, just as if you were to cram Tuesday's plain space with Neapolitan ice cream.

Watch out! Here comes a bevy of *l*'s: *la-la,* ancient and honorable euphemism for lavatory, but also, in your case, a survival from your soprano singing while on your pot; *Linna* (Linda), of whom you were fond and whom you still call on to materialize from where she is in kindergarten; *lollee,* minus the "pop," which you bear aloft as a mace of office or bang with to make gongs out of trays or employ as unshiftable bookmarks (the sticks of devoured *lollees* always serving you, like the little sticks of Alfred Jarry's pataphysical King Ubu, for poking in people's ears); and *lock,* for all the clocks you hold to your ear as other and older children hold transistor radios.

lam (lamp) I've just remembered, a word you utter with some adoration. Into all *lams* you stare as if you are an Aldous Huxley cleansing the doors of your perception (the brighter the better; all things bright are beautiful to you); and, nightly, you position yourself before the bank of studs in the hallway and tap them in and out like a long distance operator having trouble in getting a Moon number or a jet pilot working his selector switches with impeccable cool. Night after night you hit on the same correct selection of lights; what goes before is mere flamboyant prowess. Figuratively, lamp is any source of light, including sun and moon and television screen, which is why, I suppose, you occasionally race out to effect the big switch-off that dooms us to TV light while you survey the lustrous gray of the dimmed room with the measured exhilaration of an astronaut just stepped out into his first moon crater. But with strobes do not trifle; loving light as you do, though, a career in TV or as a skiing in-instructor would be fine: arc lamps or snow dazzle would suit you mighty fine, with all the rest of us cowering in our Polaroid cool-rays. *Lorv* (love) you bay at us with clowning relish and *leg* you murmur as if it's an obscenity. That's *l*.

Man-dee, Mamm-a, momter, more, mou! It's almost a sentence: Mandy asks her mother for more thermometer in the mouth (as distinct from thermometer underarm or rectally). Your own name you finally learned after about a year's repetitious calling of it into the audio trainer that boomed it back to you through massive black-rubber earphones that always made you look like a goggle-eyed midget wireless man sending an SOS from a sinking ship. *Mandee* or *Mandee* you utter with a prideful almost reverential deepening of your voice, making the pause (when you make it) dramatic: from middle C to G below. You were five before you knew you had a first name and now, two years later, you are just beginning to acknowledge your surname. *Mamma, Mamm-a,* however, you've had longer and you now snap it out with a jussive briskness, especially when forcing upon your mother a plate of food you've lost interest in. Your adaptation of thermometer I think brilliant, whether you see the *thing* as a silver-thin cigarette or not. Fetched home from school when you were ill, you kept showing us your armpit, where we searched for a rash—something wrong. No rash, and nothing else; it was where school had put the *momter,* and you wanted a repeat. Then you learned the word, and you ask for *momter* now whenever you feel off-color; which, considering your handicap, compels your doctor into a near-veterinary role (you haven't the words to tell him what you feel any more than, say, Boyd has), is a useful home signal when other signs are lacking. Unless, frivolous girl, you just want to play at doctors. When the doctor arrives, you at once roll up your blouse and undervest; you know what sickness is, and resignation too. *More,* which *mou* asks for more often than Oliver Twist ever did, is a bizarre word which now means only what it should (either a curt aside or a gourmand bellow, with never so much as a "please"—word you don't have); it used to mean pop or lemonade or beer even. Asking for more pop more often than for more of anything else, you built association into identity—at least, until you began to use "pop" seriously and, later, coined *beebee.*

nose you sing when you itemize your face, but also still use for elephant (having almost got that word, you spurned it at the last moment). *Nail* is on the finger but not yet under the *pomper. Ny* is nine, and *no,* always a violent exclamation, you conduct with much pseudo-pedagogical finger wagging and, rather too often, iterate for ten minutes as if seeking to wear the word down to discover the secret printed into its lining, and all the time mock-slapping yourself. Deaf children are not angels, as you and I know; but if to forbid you is to drive you into obsessed echolalia (as many as a hundred *nos* a minute in mimicry or parody.), I'll use only my periphrasis, "We don't do that," except for when you are desperately wrong—as when on the verge of discovering electricity or brutally modifying the physique of innocent strangers (unless they have jeered at you, and then I'd equip you with a lead pipe myself). Always, we know although you don't, one should speak to deaf children in sentences and not batter them with single words (your own preference for isolates is acute enough as it is). So, not like the Alice who in *Henry V* instructs the princess Katherine in one foreign word at a time (*col,* nick; *coude,* bilbow), I muster unilateral whole sentences to hold your attention, you, to whom the sentence is as foreign as trigonometry or Peshtu. All the same, you watch: see us moving our mouths at length, only six inches from your two microphones; and you see, I hope, *see-hear,* something of the combinations, whether the matter happens to be "The car is ready outside," "This is potato salad," or (as sometimes, when I'm uptight) "Imagination wasn't given to us to use for mental Xerox-copying; it's there for purposes of play, invention, and exploring." Such are the verbal combos used to sell you on a very useful habit, called speech, you must acquire for keeps.

Ollie is what you decreasingly call Boyd; *oo* means pretty (although not when it's part of *hot-oo*); and *oo-ah*, oral version of a vertical hump, means "slide," a word you now are converting into *zlar*—said with almost feral zeal. Whether you've rings on your fingers and bells on your toes, you shall have not music but slides wherever you go, preferably blue and yellow like the big one at school, or red and yellow like the lesser one on the grass at home, there to be slid down, walked up, lain full length on right way up or upside down, sung to, assaulted, swabbed down and, of course, reproduced in acre upon acre of dismembered cardboard, two-dimensional or three-, and mounted in all rooms among the bric-a-brac of daily living. Whatever the cost in Brobdingnagian confetti, portions that leopards and nest-building jackdaws reject, and scissor-sore thumbs, your obsession with slides must be fed. *Wooooo!* you call during descents real or imagined, *wooooo!* And *wooooo!* we go with you. As for *out*, it means "out on foreign territory" where you may have to compete for monopoly of the slides, and never outside in your own garden or between the door and the gate. *Out* that you own is part of the pleasuredome into which you have converted an entire house.

Any *pl* you just uncritically worship in plane-chant serenade. Planes get bought, built, and broken here at something like emergency speed while my head buzzes from sniffed-in glue and my fingers ache from clamping joints together while the glue sets and none of the nail files have any rough left, such has been the trimming and chamfering of ill-combining parts which the machines in the factory have botched. *Pl!* we cry as your Zero meets my Executive head on; *wooooo!* as they miss and climb away toward Picasso's Old Woman and the lamp whose pull string you professonally snap at three-week intervals. Planes readymade and planes built from kits, planes folded from stiff paper (oh, remind me to buy you that book about them which has an appendix of press-out cardboard ones), planes in silhouette from every magazine and box lid we can find, planes drawn with *pen* (which also means "crayon" and "pencil"), and planes which are just stiffened hands with uptilted thumbs—these await our command, a mini-SAC of the living room. Now:

PLAR is the Bandaid you apply for kicks.

PLEE is the word *we* say to *you*, pretty-please you spurn.

POMPER is to hammer as hammerhead is to shark (already "done").

POO is what you DO, but very irregularly, in the *la-la*.

POOL, not a game but where, in which, you bathe in summer. It's plastic.

POON is any spoon not born in anyone's *mou*.

POP is potable and nothing to do with music, art, etc.

And PRI-Y, not a crossword clue, but "pretty"—keen, swish, dead neat, or overpoweringly gaw-juss. Let's trail these lines behind our planes like streamers, although if you aren't careful that last one will wrap round your throat and your airscrew, your windthroat and your corkscrew, like the conjoined scarves of all the Oxford colleges, including if you land downwind even the holy ones where the beds are cross-shaped and you have to bring your own vinegar, the toilets like thundering caldrons lodged in peat bogs owned by the

Words for a Deaf Daughter 103

Baskerville Hound-Dog—You'll soon have more *p*'s than *b*'s, but they can't caution you to watch your *p*'s and *q*'s (you've no *q*'s anyway). Just "be natural," which my mother writes in the autograph books of her music pupils. There's a jazzy commotion in the air, so let's have a song as if the ICBM's were raining down and we've sheltered in a revolving door, you with your fair-weather umbrella up and me with my broad psychedelic flowerpower tie bound like a blindfold over my eyes:

Gaw-juss
Frab-jus
Lan-gous-
  tine

Scrum-ptious
Lus-cious
Tan-ger-
  ine (*Wait for it now, wait for it*)

Treach-rous
Up-as
At-tro-
  pine (*Wait wait wait*)

Quinquireme!
Quincunx!
Quoit! (*Here we go now—*)

CWINCWIREEM!
CWINCUNX!
CWOIT!

I met a man
  whose brain-pan
    it ran
      with

> tan
> bran
> roundabout the garden
> like a teddy-bear (HERE PULL
> FACE OF BEAR)
> one step, two-step
> and tickle you under
> there! *Bo-a!*

I am putting you on *rounabou,* a miraculously long word to come from you, but it's one of our main games, for which you find time in the midst of all our most urgent projects—painting lollipops with poster color, assembling (out of a cardboard certificate tube and yards of Scotch tape) something like a water cannon, invigilating the middle distance, irrigating the kitchen floor to see what it will grow, even exploring topmost shelves while standing on two rickety stools. *Rounabou* soothes you just as much now as it did when you were two, a sport less hectic than *bo-a* or upstairs chasing with me as old Nosferatu, my fangs fresh from the dentist, my blood supply woefully short. How many thousand times you've played *rounabou!* It never palls or fails, and you don't care for innovative variations either. Spread-eagled over my knees, you detonate with mirth at the tickle after a suspenseful and delicious agony during the *one, two* steps. But *rounabou* also means carousels, full-size or miniature (like the French one you have with, still inside the base, sugared almonds caked with sand and salt of the sea), their only drawback being friction: they are not a *perpetuum mobile*. The big ones shiver and halt and then, while you gesticulate and fume as if the world has come to an end—thwarted equestrian or space pilot that you are —someone fumbles among his coins to purchase the lurch-off that renews your spell. Or, with miniature ones, someone has to do the spinning while you peer at the wooden dolls in the chairs like a medic at the window of a decompression chamber, alert for panic or collapse, and inspector-faced. (You are also beginning to use *rounabou* to distinguish skirts, which go *round* you, from pants, which you think don't.)

Sibilants, for you, only just exist, and you give only the merest touch of *s* to *sheep, shoe, smoke, sock,* and *soon,* much preferring to say none of these words except *shoe.* Utility words that easily decline into *ee, oo,*

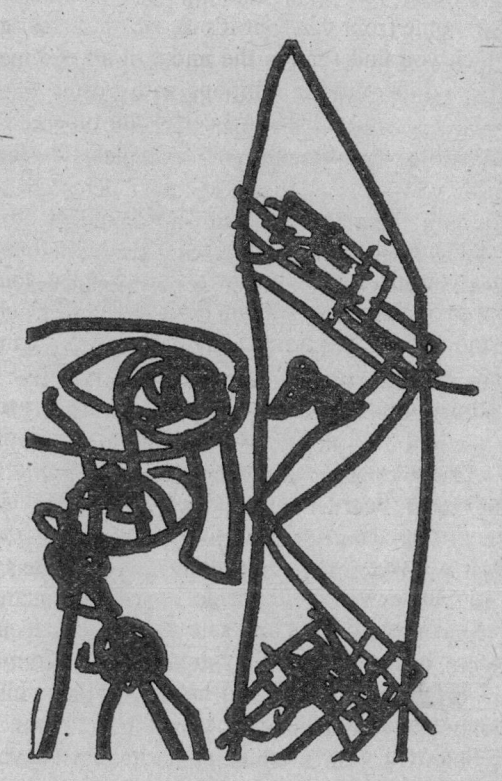

"zlide..."

mo, zo, and *zoo* because they don't interest you, whereas into *slide,* an *s*-word that excites you, you fit a buzzing engine to give it speed: *zlar, zlide*. Buzz, buzz, as Hamlet says; all the world's a *zlide*. *Zix* and *zeven* you sometimes enjoy, but in removing the *s*'s from "seesaw" you manage to introduce a donkey into it: *eeaw*.

All your *t*'s are close to *d*, but how could anyone expect you to know how to pull your tongue back from the one to make the other? "Teeth" become *dtee,* nonetheless, which is in itself a tribute to the accuracy of your lip-reading. Having tried to decipher for myself those twitching, pouting, springing, elongating pairs of chicken livers called lips, which curl into a new shape almost before the present one's complete, I feel defeated for you—except that you aren't defeated at all. If we mouth things to you, with no sound at all, you speak them back to us with more precision than we have a right to expect and in deftly modulated tones. When you do that, it's as if the blueprint has become the working model right there before our eyes. Some of your sounds, though, are involuntary, like your Arab's burp which you know by its vibration (as you know those other noises you make during waits in quiet waiting rooms); insouciant eructating that is a law unto itself, like the reputedly superior beauty of the women of Barcelona or Memphis or Nottingham ... wherever you want, it's a notion as unverifiable as your wind is free, and every bit as unarguable about as those consummate lists, in *The Pillow Book of Sei Shonagon,* of Things Which Make One's Heart Beat Faster, of Things Which Are Hard to Say, of Outstandingly Splendid Things, of Very Dirty Things. Let's not quibble: for Things Which Some People Think Embarrassing While You Laugh, thank you. And, in return, to fatten out your *t*'s:

teetotum (to spin and win with); *teff* (the Abyssinian cereal); *teg* (a young sheep); *tegmen* (a covering), *tegular* (to do with tiles)—such are the *t* words you may never have, and what's the loss so long as we have dictionaires to cold-store the needless arborescence of vocabulary? You'll manage as long as you can rouse your big sister from her pre-breakfast sleeps by thumping up the stairs, like an irate farmer, barking her name in mounting crescendo until, splendor of splendors, you site your mouth at her ear and again sound off: *Tiya,* TIYA! And Tina wakes. *Toe-ee* (Tony) is another absent friend of the kindergarten to whom you signal vocally while busying your hands with something else. What's in a name? What?—about a year's coming to terms with it and rolling it round your mouth until you've found the most comfortable way of saying it, as you did with *tsin* for chin, *twev* (which you developed from *dwelve* through *dwel* and *twerv*) and *dren* for train.

For *u,* of which you have no stock at all, let's bring up *v: vor* and *vy* (4 and 5), which still wouldn't be much if we couldn't call on the *w* (these three are one another's aliases anyway). *Wall* and *wee* you understand but don't much bother to say, whereas *wodbar,* which you occasionally weaken to *wortar* with a disingenuous giggle, is an exultant statement of ownership, while *wat* is not only "wet" but also your version of your surname (Mandee Wat). *Wim* for swim is new, as is *wynd,* your only true verb, and therefore given heavy use: to wind is to wind clocks, of course, to peel out those Polaroid snaps, to stir or whip mixtures in a bowl, to turn a screwdriver on a screw, to switch on the TV, to sharpen a crayon in a pencil sharpener, to adjust a thermostat, to peel a potato, to spread covers on a bed with a furling motion, to slide curtains, to open the door by twisting knob or turning key. . . . It is as if you've just discovered the wheel that makes the world go round, and *wynd* is the summary verb for all appropriate handlings of things. So, to wind an egg, I suppose, would be to fry, boil, or poach it, and to count is to *wynd* round from *wun* through all your fingers.

Winding up our lexicon won't take long. *Yap, yaw, Yayee, yoap, yop, yummay*—being Scotch tape, saw (real, Hong Kong half-real, or cardboard cutout), myself, soap, "stop!" (to be said when plonking your thumb on the little ball on top of one of your roundabouts), and pacifier. One word, *yabut,* you have evolved from watching us say, "What is it?" That's what it means. I point at something and, at once, you look me in the eyes and ask, *yabut?* with the stress on the first syllable. *Zix* and *zeven* and we are done. In fact we were done before them, having had them already. There are too, of course, numerous hortatory ululations, which perhaps don't *mean* at all but are mere mouth work for a dull moment or a cold winter, as are your various sibylline pointings. One sound, however, a high-pitched menacing warble, means scissors and is usually reinforced with the index and middle fingers of one or both hands flicking in the manner of scissor blades. All the variants of *oi, oi-ya, ee-ya,* and *ee* I haven't, I'm sure, quite mastered, and soon might not need to anyway; you use them less and less, except on the bad days when you regress to three, mostly on account of constipation ("Has she *been* at school?" We never know; you never tell us anything like that.)

Getting on for a hundred words, then, this vocabulary of yours comes to between an eighth and a ninth of C. K. Ogden's Basic English although, I suspect, his criterion—"What other words do we need in order to define something when we do not already know the right word for it?"—makes you something of a hit-and-run artist, a beach-comber, a swagman, a linguistic gypsy. Sometimes, Canute-like, you bid the tides of language retreat; at other times, like Boadicea, you drive your knife-wheeled chariot over the living bodies of even the words you know. Half your words begin with the labials *b, m, p, w,* or with *d,* sounds which look identical to the reader of lips. You eye our mouths and probably our minds as well, but as Robert Louis Stevenson remarked in a reverie on character making in fiction, "we can put in the quaint figure that spoke a hundred words with us yesterday by the wayside; but do we know him?" We know you well, but not well enough, you quaint and jaunty, beautiful, demonic creature, but not through conversational exchange, which here figures as a paradise neither lost nor regained but just never opened up. Our "talk," such as it is, is almost symbolical stuff, expressionistic, varying between relentless decoding and slow-motion, dramatic enunciating. No wonder that, out of thin air, comes a song, *Listen to the hearing aids,* as they whistle and whine out of unison, cramming your ears with static from invisible mockingbirds who use you as their own private robot.

Yet, Canute, Boadicea, Mistress of Mini-Babel, you and your handicap don't always win, however little your aids seem to give you, however much at times you behave like your handicap's own *aide:* the tides shove in upon you, the maimed language gets back on its feet, the meaningful phonemes float clear of the babble, and, confronted with a sheet and cards each bearing the same words—for example, *watch, bike, plane, pool, slide, swing, brella*—you match word to word perfectly without much hesitation. The money denominations on stamps you rediscover on the faces of clocks, and now you count out wrestlers and boxers on TV along with the referee. Only a ghoul would write you off, but only a criminal optimist would think you are going to have an easy time of it with *any* mode of spelling, with the abstractness of words, and all those necessary but inaudible and nearly invisible sounds—not to mention microphone friction and the special dangers that catarrh and sinusitis bring for you. Even within the enclave of the multiple handicapped, life isn't *that* easy for you; and, as for outside it, where you have a right to go, you will have to be a lioness in the streets once your present utter lack of self-consciousness has gone, as it no doubt will. Some of the nineteen-year-old deaf, aware that they sound uncouth, are shy to speak; and yet you, whose deafness is a symptom of something else that is wrong, long always to be out and about. I hope you always will.

One study comes to my mind on a mongol boy (IQ 24) who, it was supposed, had one word only: *pie*. Yet, during a special course of speech stimulation, he exhibited a vocabulary of 102 words. And my mind moves on from that case to the extremely distant tenth-century Japan of Sei Shonagon, lady-in-waiting to the Empress Sadako. If Sadako hadn't passed on a gift of paper to her, would Sei Shonagon ever have begun the journal she kept in the drawers of her wooden pillow? I intend to furnish you with an endless supply of paper, then, and fiber pens to match. I promise to resume and, as they say in Spain, analphabetically. Just think (a thought to tide you through), when you settle for your first pair of Levi's, you'll be choosing among sand, silver gray, pewter, jade, olive, whiskey, charcoal, bronze, navy, loden, antelope, wheat, banana, pumpkin, and hot chocolate, all colors having copper rivets at the strain points. Have them all, for, after all, at the beginning of our lexicon I stalled with colors because I was shy to get to words, and—as the old miner told young Levi Strauss in around 1850 when Levi was selling his tough fabric to tent and wagon makers, "pants don't wear a hoot up in the diggins. Caint git a pair strong enough to last no time." One hundred fifty million pairs later, all those colors await your pleasure. Out of *these* diggins, now, let us go. The gold is dug.

Words for a Deaf Daughter 111

Hothothot superhot stoppress postscript or it would be 'cept for my own lousy memory, its banks low as a neap tide: ADDENDA! *angoo* thankyou, *dk* duck, *ear* ear, *fi* fish, *ow-moo* cow, and God alone knows how many more, it's coming out of my ears all the time I'm thinking about you, you'll beat us all yet. *EEEeeeeee-eee*, ish-ish. ANGOO, Angoo, angoo.

Here it nearly all is; I feel like Midas at the Mint: angoo appul Aroo bababababa bar Be beebee bir blun bo boa! boat Bobbee boid boo brella brow bu burr bye-bye car cig dayn dey ding dk dog dog-woof doo dree dren dtee dwel dwelve ear e'bow ee ee! ee-aw e'even ee-ya eigh ellow e-oe eye fi file fur fy gawyee gibig har hawz hot-oo! hwingh ie-gree ish-ish kool la-la lam leg Lina lock lollee lorv Mamma Mandee mirroe mo mom-ter moon more mou nail no nose ny Ollie oo oo-ah oi oi-ya! out ow-moo pen pl plar pomper poo pool poon pop pri-y pun rav rounabou ry s-s wi ngh Tiya Toe-ee tsin twerv twev var vor vy wall wat Wat wee wim woh! worbar wortar wun wynd yabut yap yaw Yayee yoap yop yum-may zeven zhee zho zhoo zix zlar zlide zmo zo zoo zwingh

And *angoo* once again, my head's a-spin; I think you just said please.

5.

Arabian Prelude to a Night

Resuming in a blue-checked washable thing called a Treasurobe (no doubt, like Long John Silver's parrot, it once belonged to Robinson Crusoe-Kreutznaer), I snatch a look at the newspaper. Solray flame-effect electric fires, it seems, are so real they actually do fool people; Joanie Jaynes was *really* fooled, she tried to boil an egg on one. By their illusions ye shall know them.

See how it is when I'm trying to wake up? Your hair is very long in the A.M., before we draw it tight into two pony tails held by modish butterflies of white-spotted blue ribbon. Blue? No, almost black; it's hard to know in the half-light of the day or the double-brightness of the kitchen strip lighting.

It was 84° F. in Bermuda yesterday.

To wake thoroughly up, just as to get off to sleep, you wag your head violently from side to side, a perfect rhythm to brush teeth to, and thus (I think) throw more blood into the narrowest capillaries in your brain; it tells the back-of-the-neck muscles to look lively while your hair streams back and forth like a mane of white raw cotton, a soft flog on my face when you stretch out beside me in bed for the first five minutes of being awake on a school morning, or, when you stand downstairs, a fickle indoor wind that sets Nosferatu on

Words for a Deaf Daughter

his line gently bouncing in mid-air, a preening devil in gangrene colors. Eat your cornflakes; pack that egg away. *Beebee!*

The three envelopes you flung at me ten minutes ago enclosed three bills, but the big packet is a follow-up to your request last year for information on Bermuda (which you sliced up during a wet, blustery, *Wuthering-Heights*-type afternoon). You are invited to go again at the going rate for single girls: JET IN COMFORT TO TALC-SOFT SANDS AMERICAN PLAN AND AIR CONDITIONING. Even the ice buckets stand in yet bigger ice buckets which stand in bigger bigger . . . the whole island *sits* in a mammoth ice bucket manufactured in Houston. *You* take the leaflets, all pastel littorals and bicycled-over greensward and expensive ultramarine sea, and *I*'ll have the envelope—two sheets, once I've slit it, with a tough, grainy surface within, so it's almost like using a stylus over soft buff wood. For this resuming letter to y— *Ak-aruk!* Sorry, it's that so-called relaxed throat of mine climbing into the back of my nose (the cure being to gargle with port wine, but not, surely not, before the sun is up). Fumbling in a cloth inlet in Treasurobe, I come up with a pellet in foil just as you stab an egg that has waited too long and will not ochre-run. If I go out I promise to block my mouth with plaster of Paris. Now drink your *beebee* down.

"*Beebee!*" Empty cup slams down; spoon levitates, bearing with it my grandmother's initials, V.N.

"Mandy is going out in the car to school!"

"*Koo-ool? Koo-ool!*" That moving finger writes in mid-air, bold serif.

"Yes. School."

"*Ding?*" Hand-simulating it.

"No-ooooo. Out in the car to school."

"*Bo?*" A perfunctory *heil*-Escalator, right-handed.

"No, no. Not bo, out—"

"*Kool! Kool!*" You smell at my face to identify the aroma of the thing I'm sucking.

"Man-dee!"

You want one too. If I can find one I'll give you one. Now you have one and at once spit it out onto your egg, like a black incisor on the ploughed-up yolk. *See,* I begin to say, but you have gone off to brush your teeth, wee, be dressed in blue and white and have all that hair lashed down and then, as you begin to develop on your sleek and minty face the sort of expression old Delius must have had when the sun coming up lit on his eyelids, put on the canvas double harness (white for girls, blue for boys) that holds in two silk purses the two sow's ears you have to wear.

Without even looking down, you switch on, rolling both 0-1-2-3-4-5 control wheels to 5 while we test each earpiece to see if the squeal is steady. A big, preparatory smile with your jaw thrust high as if to reassert your expertise, and you fix the transparent plastic earpieces in where they belong, tap once on each of the flesh-tinted buttons that come almost flush with the lobes, and immediately begin chanting to yourself while your hands (a touch lurid from purple nail varnish imperfectly mopped off with remover while you slept) check the leads and the tiny plugs which we ourselves test nightly when we unsnap earpiece from button and clean the sound-bringing holes with pipe cleaners and, if necessary, replace your tiny batteries. During the rest of the day, at school and then at home again, you will adjust your equipment as you want, nonchalantly replacing an earpiece dangling from its lead after you've buffeted it loose in play, irritably stabbing a plug back home. Sound, at maximum, is the land of heart's desire you're fully wired for.

And then you go, a schoolgirl of a special kind, unable to report to us on the day's doings but usually bearing home the signs of them: teeth marks on a

Words for a Deaf Daughter

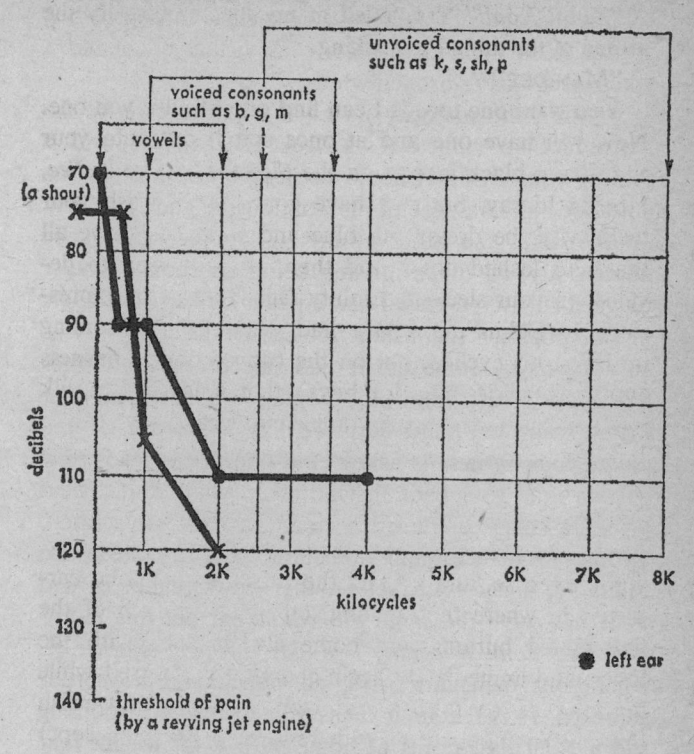

[Audiogram showing frequency response from 1K to 8K kilocycles on x-axis and decibels from 70 (a shout) to 140 (threshold of pain, by a revving jet engine) on y-axis. Labels indicate vowels, voiced consonants such as b, g, m, and unvoiced consonants such as k, s, sh, p. Data plotted for left ear.]

"Sound, at maximum . . ."

wrist; variegated poster color on your clothes and skin; or, more explicit, on Friday when your homework book comes with you, a fiber-pen sketch of what you did, together with a caption in ITA: "Wɛɛ went tω the ʃhops." Or: "Wɛɛ paented." It is a vacuum-quiet house without you and the conversations behind your back are very much about you: unending speculations as to what you are doing (what agile stunt you'll perpetrate today), what you'll do with your lunch, your spending money, your broad fists. No one babies you at this junior level, so I know *they*'re all man enough to give the pants of some of you a rinse through when wet or knobbly, and to receive as virtual phonemes a whole schoolday's broken winds.

At four, the majority go back into the care of the house mothers (unless it's a weekend) and you, with a few of your living-at-home contemporaries, sit in the entrance hall in a pose of meretricious languor, one foot on the floor, the other swung up on the other knee immodestly, all that's missing being an ebonite holder plugged with a red-ended black-paper Balkan Sobranie.

Two popsicles the instant you invade the car.

Your hair's come adrift and one of the butterflies has come apart; your blue panties are down to your knees; your left-hand earpiece has a splodge of red paint; your harness is askew and one of the leads now winds round your back instead of up your front. Sweat prints, a smear of pink ice cream, a nail-pale scratch, all on your face; and somehow you are steaming, ramming, ahead with yet another day's school behind you: not quite the same girl who went out this morning. *I've done it again, I've got through another,* is what your demeanor says, all punch and boisterous self-help. A full hour it takes you to unwind, zooming through all the rooms at home with a fat ice in your paw and the aids whistle-crackling as if you are tuned in to transmissions from North Borneo. But: two girls came to hold hands with you when you got there this morning; your Pakistani touched you a furtive goodbye. You have been social. You have won again. Now you can cut Bermuda up with your best scissors.

If only there *were* the perfect place; if only *there* were the perfect place, only half real with Prussian blue umbrellas marching muffle-spiked so as not to bruise the flour-soft salmon-pink sand and the sea turned up loud so you could hear it and even, way out, old brine shrimp *Artemia salina,* swiveling his belly ever upward because he steers by the direction of the falling light, *en route* to lodge in your hand so you'll think he's the sea creature long lost from 101 Toys in One Box that came rattling in in the mail a Christmas ago, and then he swims off in a sulk, you bumped one of his semispherical compound eyes and he's now like the cross-eyed double-seeing lion in *Daktari*. . . . Good thinking, Artemia Salina, you know your Francis Bacon all right, who said, "The subtlety of Nature transcends in many ways the subtlety of man." Yes, but Confucius he say, No shrimp transcend subtly or otherwise unsubtle bang-bash-clout-clamp-clutch-caress of Manda hand; only Boyd.

Beg pardon, I intend no caricature; it all comes of your being away during the day, just as that bulldozed-watercress feeling comes from your being home at weekends. It's hard, considering your extraordinary multiple personality and the unusual feats you perform in so everyday a way, *not* to mythologize you in your absence: aggrandize you, magnify you, Alexander-the-Great you, Eric-the-Red you, Ivan-the-Terrible you, Joan-of-Arc you, Robin-Hood you, Louis-XIV you, Marco-Polo you, Last-of-the-Mohicans you, Paul-Revere you.

Helen-Keller you.

You stare at me as if I'm simple, wanting to inflict on you prowesses, gifts, knacks, and transubstantial wizardries you don't even know about as first-hand hokum. Why tell me all this? you scoff; it's telling told by an idiot. Well, I just see how the ingenuities of your rituals and your games might catapult you into something else: your mantras into a Veda that is beyond all encyclopediae, Britannicae or Americanae; your infatuation with water, its tricks, its hydraulic kinks, into a post-Noachic flood; your flawless rocking into a new form of stand-up sleep; your private words into a basic Cosmispeak transmittable to Mars; your middle-distance observations into the first eyeball accounts of freaked-out intergalactic visitors who have invisibly been here since the first Knight was photographed while being so dubbed by a British monarch with a sword, all the anti-imperialist newspapers publishing the picture as one of an execution: Queen Beheads World Traveler. . . . I mean, Manda, unicorns and manticores and centaurs and phoenixes and gryphons and dragons and Rumpelstiltskin and Beauty and the Beast and Rip Van Winkle who heard the thunder of Hendrick Hudson and his crew bowling ninepins. The ground glass of optical illusion is all I'm left with if I try explaining. I'll lay it all at the door of a mysteriousness about you which many would think irrelevant beside your learning to solve a quadratic equation, parse Genesis' first sentence, sing an exact Middle C, but which I myself have learned from and which your rituals defy us to explore.

Soon after wolfing your home-from-school meal—sausages and eggs and French-fried potatoes made almost inedibly tangy with great globs of Düsseldorf mustard, or a roast chicken which you squat on the floor with and tear apart red-handedly where it sits on the coffee table, or meat pies that you lackadaisically eviscerate while tossing the pastry away like refuse—you race outside to swing and slide, heedless of weather. And someone has to follow, not only to shove the swing seat and chase you up the slide's ladder, but, if it's wet out (*wat*), to site a pad of cardboard at the slide's foot so you won't muddy your pants, or to peel away from either structure offending leaves and blades of grass which the weather has plastered on the struts and which provoke you into a special Get-Off-Mah-Laynd anger. The same person must also take outside with him a supply of Kleenex to wipe your boots with, and your knees and the rungs of the ladder. Mud offends you so much that if it's on your boots (especially the white ones) you will not walk or, if on the ladder, will not mount or, if on the swing seat, will not sit. It's just another of your contradictions: in many ways a lord of misrule, you are also a demon for neatness, and you achieve the latter by subjecting us and the world to cast-iron procedures, to vary which is to invite a relentless onslaught. Only one variation in a hundred gives you pause and then wins your patronizing smile that acknowledges ingenuity without encouraging further experiment. Lobster turning red when cooked is exactly the sort of constant which, on a whim, you'd like to change, then keep it that way; and heaven help whoever could not revise the natural-culinary universe to that extent, once your mind was made up.

In from the garden, you break into a rock, left foot to right with the insteps rising an inch only, until one of us interrupts and rocks with you, making it social. At this you giggle, having, for all your compulsions, some idea of what adults are and are not likely to do. Nonetheless, you will always join in if we offer to rock; indeed, you come and stand on my shoes if I so much as shuffle feet to vary the position I'm standing in. The merest sign and you are heavily on the front of my feet, and the pair of us are going: left-right, left-right, a rhythm that has now worked its way so far into my system I now quite regularly rock in my own right—in my office, in the bathroom, waiting for planes or trains. A bizarre sight it must be, an apparently grownup square swaying with mechanical regularity as if alienated from all conventional time-killing techniques and, being incapable of exact interpretation, dismissed as drunk, spastic, or a victim of combat fatigue. Whatever onlookers happen to think, they don't realize three things: I've been brainwashed; so far as I know, I rock quite deliberately (whereas some folks don't know when they're finger tapping and toe waggling or giving out with a twelve-tone hum); and to rock is soothing anyway, almost as much as Madeira, a neck rub, or midnight movies watched but expendably forgotten come the next day.

Then the chase with heathen faces, you forever exhorting me to leers more fiendish than I've yet accomplished and my only recourse being illustrated books on gargoyles, on masks in the Congo and New Guinea, or the simple addition to my face of Kleenex ropes dangling from the nostrils, celluloid fangs that droop down onto my chin, and rubber masks from which a bleeding eyeball is dangling without actually being loose; as well as—tricky—cottonwool beards and sideburns unfortunately overlapping with Santa Claus the Beard. Hooting for innocuous horror, you reveal a taste for the gross, the grotesque, the garish, with which I sympathize more than many people would, I having always been willing to trade a hundred Gainsboroughs for one Goya, five hundred Wyeths for one Brueghel, a thousand Manets for one Bosch. I'm not, I'm sure, the only student who repeatedly fell asleep, trying to read the anemic drivel of the Galsworthys of this world when, damnit, there was Rabelais and Nashe and Joyce to go at! And then Rimbaud, Gogol, and Beckett. End of name dropping except to recommend, as a man on his children, Henry Miller. It's bath time, once an almost open-ended procedure entailing (you recall?) a preliminary tarantella in the nude, then water sports with a host of floating toys including water pistols, long plastic bottles, and the three-foot doll, and interminable conclusions when you had to station a dozen articles *just so* on the bath tidy, wash the soap and then redeposit it in the dish of water where it dissolved overnight, and arrange around the room all those paper model baths whose taps were rolled-paper tubes.

A good hour it took, all that, whereas bathing now is a perfunctory business conducted merely to keep alive a chunk of ancient fun; a ritualistic, hydropathic anti-world no longer, in which, like the children going to bed in Cocteau's film *Les Enfants Terribles,* you set every possession on the bath as they themselves set theirs on the eiderdown (as you now on *yours,* every eiderdown being a magic carpet for a perhaps irrevocable voyage). Now, sluicing only, for commonplace reasons, is enough to keep memory bright. There's only one thing of your *manie* remaining: your mother must, simply must, be in the bath with you, mostly as a victim for what seems to be your version of judo practice (you being a regular and overjoyed spectator at exhibitions of both judo and karate). But I no longer think of Lake Geneva, Loch Ness, or Marineland of the Pacific as your only possible haven. Water, for you, has found its own level; you use it, then move on, coolheaded as Archimedes.

After bath, you situate yourself in front of a large plate holding potato salad and fresh boiled ham. This waits while you devour minestrone soup and/or ravioli and settle for this purpose into your most comfortable position: flat on back in bathrobe, one leg cocked upon the other and stirring the air with that inverted slipper perched on your toes, your spoon held aloft like an assegai, a hand mirror, or a lorgnette. No wonder the front of your nightgown and robe are encrusted with a dark red that pales as it hardens. And, of course, your hair, being no longer bound, sits in the line of fire (or fallout) too, all while you flaunt the hairless pear of your *mons pubis* before the ghosts who hunch and trot on the finger-smudged TV screen; or the moon already showing while the sun dwindles.

If you've had a trying day, you'll probably have an open umbrella in one hand (no effort for strong you to hold it thus), extolling it with your eyes, much, say, as Cleopatra might if she had a chance look at her Needle on the bank of the Thames. Dawdling over food as you do, you have time to do the jigsaw of the playground (you first of all put together the pieces that make up the slide therein) or to command us to draw and cut out slides, saws, or escalators. Always the same unspoken prayer: let no piece of that puzzle be missing, or you'll raise, murder, and rebury Cain without pause until it's found or we have phoned the manufacturers at home to send in a replacement by helicopter. As soon as the puzzle is done, you bestow upon it a smile of temporarily benevolent approval (it obeyed, it occupied all of its own space) and at once dismantle it, pour it back into its plastic bag and restore it to its place in the liquor cupboard, all such places being as sacrosanct as White House parking privileges and pew protocol in Westminster Abbey. All this time, I've been forgetting to mention, you take desultory little swigs from the first round of *beebee,* a mug in either hand, one of tea, one of pop—unless you've, as the French say, "subtilized" some beer or wine. That you do not smoke during this curiously Arabian prelude to a night in which you figure as odalisque, sultana, and dancing girl all in one—I am somewhat relieved. A hubble-bubble wouldn't be a surfeiting diversion, I'm sure, any more than the various errands you undertake—to the light switches, kitchen, front door, toilet, phone, TV controls, and even the bookshelves—distract you from your main purpose of not going to bed. Always detected at it, you're never made to pay. Time gained is one of your forms of contraband.

All this time, too, we have been keeping tabs on your mood, alert for the moment when you lie full length behind your mother on the sofa and eat your apples. Once or twice you come to where I sit bemused and ask for *rounabou* or sit on my knee for a song:

> Where's that little Manda gone?
> Where's that little Man-da?
> Where's that little—

> There's that little—
> *Here's* that little Manda!

A voluptuary grin from you confirms that you know where you are, and we repeat the song with variants, but always to the same brisk jog of a rhythm. Whoever gets up to move out of the room, you follow at speed, administering little valedictory slaps upon the hands of those remaining behind or heel tapping such of the furniture as has also stayed put. The world and we begin to drift once you are in position, abstractedly gnawing, and the lull sometimes lasts half an hour and even longer when, very tired after a day of steady brainwork, you fall asleep with a slice of apple in hand. Then it comes to carrying you upstairs. Otherwise, you utter one *beebee,* a deferential murmur but just as unquestionable as a factory whistle or a sonic boom. This means the evening is over, no matter what anyone else wants to do, and the milky bedtime drink has to be prepared. It is, and in the meantime you have probably gone up to lie on the bed and wait, your eyes on the ceiling and, on your face (if you are well), a look of beatific amusedness or (if you are unwell) of *rerum horror* that doesn't belong to a child at all.

In bed, propped up alongside your mother on pillows and some by now rather spoiled-looking velvet cushions, you seem royally secure; and it is now that the rituals become baroque. Once the umbrellas of the day have been hung on any available handle, and the toy watches and paper slides and plastic aircraft have been aligned on the dressing table like offerings on an altar for Narcissus, and the rubber sheet beneath you (just in case) has been groomed straight, you take the *beebee* mug, rotate the spoon, and wait for us to begin with the three dogs who dominate this pantomime. The first of these, in pink plastic, whom you have fed from your bedtime mug for at least two years, we have to balance upside down along the bridge of your nose while you more or less hold your breath. Since he's an ear missing, you have to tilt your head to allow for his imbalance, but you strike the right attitude at once and close your eyes. Now the other two dogs, which collapse altogether when we press the bottom plate up into the base and spring up rigid again when we release it, come wobbling and mowing toward your forehead, making mock sallies nearer and nearer until one or the other dislodges the pink dog and you chuckle with husky glee at his fall.

At this point you take a gulp of *beebee* and feed all three dogs, who in turn tap your lips with theirs: milk kisses, until we set the odd-dog-out upon your nose again and dislodge him once again. Once more you feed the dogs, offering them a full spoon to sip from or plunging their heads into the mug. Here I must confess to having done something underhand, something you noticed but decided not to protest about. One of the two dog-toppling dogs lost literally his head and I used some wadding to jam it onto his tail, so we now have a very long neck and only a short tail, and a head where no head ever was before. You scrutinize this Dr. Moreau—like shift with constant but cordial astonishment, caught (no intention of mine) between your love of the grotesque and your love of uniformity. Two years ago, I think, you would have flung the deformed dog from you in a fit of rampant perfectionism, made me feel like someone Boris Karloff should play, and insisted—in a cooler moment—on an immaculate repair. Such is the measure of the advances you have made.

We were feeding the dogs a second time. After this, you drink a few drops more yourself and then pass the mug sideways from you to whoever is there to receive it and without so much as a glance in that direction. You always assume that the world is intricately ready to cope with your next motion: you don't look, call a warning, or ask; you expect others to know the ritual as well as you do, even when you've changed it without notice. Assuming that the mug is safely out of the way, like the movement of the third floor backward, we can get on with wrapping each dog in tissues until only the muzzles show. The pink one we slide under the strap of one of a pair of plastic high-heeled shoes in which I've seen you totter about with made-up face like Alice aping the young Moll Flanders, and the other two we put to bed together in the other shoe under toe strap and heel strap respectively. Each dog "kisses" you goodnight, is kissed in return, and we rock them to sleep while you sing "see-saw" several times. That's all of that.

One pillow from behind you now goes by your side for you to hug, and you lie down, one hand tousling the hair on my head (which you haul down for just this soothing finale), the other holding your mother's left hand as anchor. Sometimes, but not often, you kiss the photographs of yourself goodnight as well, but always when I stand up with throbbing scalp and bend again, this time without kneeling, you get a fit of giggles in anticipation of the goodnight kiss. I plant this kiss, usually receiving a clout from your free hand on the way up, and then make the "sleep" sign: head sideways against hands put palms-together. After a clear *bye-bye*, another giggle or two, you "make the mustache" (as we say), which means crossing long tails of your hair along your upper lip, thus masking your eyes. Your mother sees you into the last stages, during which you do a somnolent head rock, and out I go.

Usually you are asleep within ten minutes and a faint sweat speckles your forceful, wide, and beautiful face. In the distant-seeming past, you crowded your bed inside with golliwogs and outside with an abundance of tools, jigsaw puzzles, and umbrellas. No longer: in fact, all the golliwogs have been dumped in a heap in the corner of the room, only one, the biggest (whose arrival from my mother once checked an hour-old tantrum dead in its tracks), being allowed in bed at all, and he only in the daytime; no doubt to keep goblins at bay and the big bed friendly.

At weekends that big bed becomes the scene of an elaborate levee whose centerpiece is a tray holding a teapot, some of the best china, and thin-cut, thick-buttered slices of bread which you nibble with absent-minded fervor, gazing out at the day you don't have to enter unless you want to. You may or may not decide to go *bo*-ing (Saturday) or to the swings in the playground (Sunday). If you do go out, you visit the shops and usually emerge with a clock, a jigsaw puzzle, or a plane kit hugged to you, this last to be built and parked on its nameplated Perspex stand in the increasingly chaotic airfield which the house is. Only rarely do you launch into (as only yesterday) a two-hour tirade of screaming for something you cannot have, concupiscence in its Old Testament sense feeding on its own surfeit; in that instance, a piccolo, for which you don't have the word but which, with exaggerated balloon-blowing mouth and fingers rippling along an invisible tube, you stated exactly enough. In fact there was no money, a jigsaw of an Irish fishing village (two hundred daunting, tiny pieces all looking alike) and a kit for a North American A3J Vigilante Carrier-Based Attack Bomber having taken almost all. And even if there had been, as soon as you got the piccolo you would have wanted a doll, a zip gun, a bow-and-arrow set complete with roundel targets, and even—were it available—a mini Cape Kennedy just as complete with space vehicles, Florida sunshine, and the parked cars of a hundred spectators all sucking Saturn-shaped cones of rainbow ice cream.

In the world's inexhaustible supply of dry goods you have a negligent confidence, as in my supply of money, that paltry-looking tin and paper you see people pushing across counters and having repeatedly pushed back to them (only slightly different) while you, contemptuously impatient with such folderol, ogle the goods on the shelves. The milled rims of certain coins have no more meaning for you than have bouncing checks; and yet your attitude is "fiduciary" in the widest sense, reposing on trust, so much so that you might be excused if you thought you could buy an aircraft carrier with a few *ee*s.

Entering a shop you are prehensile-bold, quick to amass on the counter the loot you fancy. You fetch it from window displays as well as distant shelves and display cases, which discomfits some of the salespeople, who seem to wonder if this mightn't develop into the latest form of conning or even holdup, but never those in the two small places with deaf owners. They shout a greeting to you, come out from behind and crouch or kneel, watching your mouth as you forbearingly say something to appease them while your empress complex gets to work through your eyes, ranging the displays for goods new and familiar. Here, you are given balloons out of fellowship; elsewhere, I think, to keep you from screaming when denied or when just covetously honking with your arm at point. One day, an oldish man in a very expensive hand-stitched suit set his palm on your head, and we thought he was deaf too; but no, he was a pediatrician who at once recognized your noises and was glad to see you out and about at your handicapped purchasing; a small envoy to conventional minds on behalf of the thousands no one ever sees or wants to see, such as your spastic contemporary at school who, having the independent determination to put on and remove her own shoes (after a few fumbles), helps *you* with yours and even, by indirections finding the direction out, hangs up your coat for you, usually at the third try, at which she smiles and then the nerve tugs the side of her mouth right up, stunting the smile but not her mood. You have learned to copy this interfered-with smile, assuming the superficies of a complaint that isn't yours, and she in turn has begun to embark on a campaign of much more extensive smiling. You, you may not know, are the ace of smilers; your days brim with joys to which you know no alternative.

Weekdays, you mix; weekends, which exhaust us but in a satisfying way, you retire like Stephen Dedalus to your tower, where you and I do two things mainly. Either we make collages with poster colors, sand, string, grit, pepper, salt, crumbs, Kleenex, coriander, and minced garlic—anything at hand—and even sometimes cut the paper and weave the good bits of the not-so-good collages over the bad and behind the good bits of the others. Always you begin with a heavy wash and then, while it's wet, paint planes and slides in that thick-pigmented, dense-cloud style that is distinctively yours. Any contribution of mine which doesn't fit into what you think your scheme is you paint out or, if it's a piece of string or something I've stuck into the viscous puddle, fish it out and sling it behind you, thus ornamenting much innocent wall or glass or bookbinding with (most often, it seems) canary yellow and Ostwald black. Thus a room becomes a kaleidoscope.

Or, when I myself do most of the work, we stick flat plastic pieces together to make three-dimensional models of Vought Corsairs (which the Japanese called "Whistling Death"), F4U's (ours always being a replica of Colonel Gregory "Pappy" Boyington's plane), Avro Ansons and Kawasaki Hiens and North American Vigilantes aforementioned and Messerschmitt Bf 109 E-3's which are venomous-nosed pencils with obsolete-looking tailplane struts. I build the tricky parts, but you fit the simpler components together, hold the fuselage halves together while the polystyrene cement sets, and then fly them with the mount stem pinched between finger and thumb. The plan and the instructions I have to read in haste, sometimes having to guess a detail of the construction, such is your impatience to see the finished article; and the transfer insignia go on almost at random, soon (anyway) to be reduced by frequent Manda-handling to a mess of stars, decals, swastikas, red suns, and sundered fuselage flashes. But there are some things that can't be taken away, such as the polyglot, quiet clinch of triumph you find on the Messerschmitt building sheet at the end of all the instructions:

IHR MESSERSCHMITT-MODELL IST NUN FERTIGGESTELLT.

VOTRE MESSERSCHMITT EST MAINTENANT TERMINE (which doesn't sound as if the same thing has been accomplished).

MODELLEN MESSERCHMITT AR NU FARDIG. Huh? How's that? Well, whoopeepee! And, just because the model *is* as complete as I shall ever have a chance to make it, I chant these linguistic marvels out to you and you laugh as if ice cream had just arrived via Telstar. We sniff styrene glue and the languages go to our heads and lift us to an ozone ceiling studded with plastic birds which, although scaled down to 1:72, breathe a condensed oxygen that has three atoms to a molecule instead of the usual two. Intoxicating, especially for grounded astronauts.

But some things we do not do. The BOX TOP PAINTING YOU CAN FRAME we cut out with scissors instead. The EXCITING FEATURES—HINGED CANOPIES—VERTICAL AND HORIZONTAL STABILIZERS THAT PIVOT—JET ENGINES REMOVABLE—we stick tight, thus dooming the crews (always for some reason Mongolian-featured) to suffocation and the plane to nil-maneuverability, its engines being impossible to service anyway. Nor do we cut out and wear the U.S. Naval Aviator Wings three-quarters of an inch across that some kits provide (BOAC gives real metal aviator's wings to children passengers, anyway, and United Arab Airlines a scarab charm to all). Moving parts don't excite us much, so we don't "cement dee locators" and other such arcane bits of plastic into the positions indicated IF UNDERCARRIAGE IS REQUIRED IN LANDING POSITION. Our air fleet never lands and never takes off, but flies non-stop until disintegration.

Nor, as we are told to, do we paint on splinter or mottle camouflages, or paint the exhausts black or dark brick red, or ever even buy the "paint-set enamel" colors of the only type we are supposed to use on any given model, or apply cement sparingly (our planes have blisters and warts), or trim excess plastic from all parts before assembling (our fuselages especially have sharp non-aerodynamic edges and open up into gaps where the fit is bad), or keep cement off the transparencies (our cockpit canopies are too smudged to be seen through). We don't even do things in the right order, so a good many instrument panels and rudder bars and other such buff's pedantries get left over and can't be installed afterward. And, worst of all, we get cement all over us, on skin and clothing and on the furniture (which it leaves with grainy pockmarks). So we have perhaps no right to send in the complaint slips to the manufacturers, not even when we find projections for which there are no slots (or vice versa), pilots too big for their cockpits or their seats, or transfers that disintegrate in the lukewarm water like the mummy's hand in those old horror films. Without knowing, I once went out with F4U accidentally transferred to the ball of my thumb and not mirrorwise either. When they cling to the skin with adhesive side outwards, you can often get them back to where they belong without tearing them; but not otherwise: better to wear them and win a colorful reputation.

Special mention in our dispatches must be made of one recent plane whose elegant lines you sit or lie and study—peruse—for hours on end, tilting it only a fraction of a degree at a time. The SUD-BAC Concorde, both French and British, flies at 1,450 miles an hour, some of it being built in Toulouse and some in Bristol. Completed sections are shipped across the Channel, and why not? There are still French onion sellers riding their bicycles around the South of England and French chefs who can't get by without Worcestershire sauce. Your own model has Air France insignia (F-BZBH) but, because we neglected to affix the windows from inside before cementing the fuselage shell together, British ventilation in the form of very fast and very unbreathable air. Which is fatal, not only for such usual reasons as decompression, but because of the heat generated during supersonic flight—why, even the cockpit windows are completely shielded once the plane has gained height. Some plane, getting you across the Atlantic so fast you can do the round trip in a day with plenty of time, depending which side you go to, to slit up your tastebuds and stomach with English coffee or to chomp on a hot pastrami on rye on a bench somewhere on Riverside Drive, to marvel at the unmortared stone walls of Derbyshire or to recoil from the honk-honk-bray-blah-blah WE'VE BEEN AND GONE AND DONE IT WE'RE TELLING YOU of American automobiles celebrating a wedding. All in a day . . . But of such marvelous voyages, and of even better ones, more later. For now, our international anthology of an air force in its naked ping-pong-ball whites, graphite grays, and nacreous greens, pinch-snouted like the fish called the muskellunge or pronged like the marlin, with not a scale of paint to peel off, holds intruders at bay and makes even the residents watch their step lest a carelessly wielded fork snap off an aerial mast, a tail-wheel unretracted, or, worse, sunder the plane's pedestal itself, thus switching on your own Rolls-Royce turbine scream.

Planes hold firm, just below slides, and below planes there's a whole range of steady devotions that proves you a connoisseur of life's footnotes; indeed, a footnote maker. You pause in the street to admire the architecture and the flagrant nuisance of a pile of horse dung, at which you point with prankish leers, sometimes almost kneeling, the better to voluptuously disapprove of it. At all cameras you snatch, heedless of levers and knobs, anxious as a superstitious Arab, Turk, or Ethiopian to haul out of its bowels the pseudo-Mandy within, whom you will then clip out in silhouette and thus rescue from the background's demonic hold. If rebuked, you draw three-foot-high caricatures of your rebukers on cardboard (sometimes even offering whoever it is a crayon with which to touch up his own image) and then pound a succession of fastidiously enunciated *Nos* at the face. Also, to soft-soap someone, you insist he draw *him*self for *you*. Given a Lord & Taylor's white summer hat with crisp and welted brim (or any other hat), you invert it and fill it with water. As if you have read T. S. Eliot on the still center of the turning world, you set your finger on the red cap in the center of the washing machine's spin disc, the finger encased in a celluloid mouthpiece from a cigarillo. Angry, or in livid expostulation, you thump your hand flat on the table, so hard the plates jump clear. Having wet yourself, you sneak away with the face of a nun hastening to an assignation and wash out your pants. You tend to be stiff-legged, flattish-footed when walking, and choose to walk that way because (I think) you enjoy the increased jolt which a footstep sends up a stiffened leg from a planked-down sole (compensatory sensation again). You very often smile in between people, directing the smile exactly to where no one is and maliciously enjoying their bafflement as, after excluding themselves from this favor, they turn round to confront—no one at all; nothing; and when they turn front again, there you are smiling ironically right at both of them, in tease, so that they dismiss what they originally thought they saw. Having an itchy back (often), you rake it with a table fork and leave it with comforting red weals. Whenever you call a thing by the wrong name, you laugh like mad, just as if it were all deliberate (it sometimes is). In similar mood you pretend to listen for the sounds (always the alarm, you do not know they tick) of your wooden or your plastic clocks, or even to wind them up. To see if anyone will try to stop you, you plunge a lollipop into a jar of factory mayonnaise and lick away the cream with stage-managed lip smacking. We have found you wearing a sanitary towel inside your pants. You possess yourself of, and stick up the front of your sweater, plastic nipple blinds which have come loose from your big sister's party dress. When busy, you tell us to keep away or out by extending your arm with a flat-palmed traffic signal on the end of it. Invariably, what was improvised yesterday—gold foil from a cigarette package wrapped round your VC-10 airliner as if Midas himself had laid on hands; crayoned cardboard clock or human faces to stick on the real clocks; birds made by tying knots in table napkins—you undo today, these things being expendable or transitory whereas others—the gargoyles on the line, the Polaroid photograph by your bed of you in a straw hat looking like a contumacious gaucho, the Hong Kong dogs who attend your goings-to-bed—are not: not yet, anyway.

Inexplicably you slap your own arm and reprimand yourself in front of mirrors. You pinch the palms of your hands as if desperate for any sensation, even pain; and then you pinch ours, anxious to give us the same pleasure. Given chance, you will address at length the cut-off heads of cod and hake, mocking through mime the dead eyes and the stiff gape of the mouths. Lost in some memory of actual fishing, you slip several jelly babies (chewable two-inch miniatures which are now manufactured with navels and are to be found in all colors but blue) into a plastic bag filled with water and wander around, showing your catch. Having, at six, allowed us to deprive you of your real pacifier, you ridicule the oral weakness of it all by shoving sugar ones into our own mouths. You lick the carving knife if you get an opportunity. You paint the ice cubes with gorgeous colors and then replace them in the freezer trays. You examine suitcases and apply Band-aids where they are worn or scored. You insist that we unpack everything on arrival back from anywhere and so hope to impede further departures. If you suspect I'm off to catch a plane or a train, you sit on a case to stop me from going. You shriek if people don't sit with their backs firmly against the backs of chairs (never, we've learned, lean forward, especially while you are eating; be waxworks instead). You raise your shoulders almost to your ears in a laconic, Marcel Marceau shrug. At all TV speakers wearing earpieces you exclaim in hardboiled sympathy, indicating, however, they should have two, not one. You hit us for not doing something you can hit us for. You scream for me to make you a cardboard slide, but won't free my hands when I try to cut. Every morning you select a prized possession to take to to school (whence few things return or return intact), and I have to pretend to begin repairing it just before you leave, which makes you almost as happy as having it with you and much happier than having it bullied away from you in the junior playground by some rapacious handicapped lout who hasn't been taught any better. Strangely, you don't practice your judo at school, almost as if you feel that only adults are strong enough to withstand it without mortal injury. To fight back is one of the things it hasn't yet occurred to you to do consistently. Perhaps we shall have to take a hint from Spain, where the matadors practice in the slaughterhouses on live cows, the head being held still, of course, by dedicated helpers who eat and breathe the bullshit mystique of it all. Never quite knowing why certain things are done to, for, or even by you, you try to be tolerant because you want to please: being bullied and having injections both hurt, and how are you to know the difference?

On second thought, though, after one experience with one sadistic dentist (a Caliban of the needle who wanted to make a fourth attempt to hit the right blood vessel and assumed that, because you are deaf, you can be punctured like a Sunday joint, being inarticulate), you find bullying easier to take. You end up, more or less, and dentists apart, in the position ascribed by John Cowper Powys to Shakespeare as "the true . . . way wherewith to take life": and that is combining "skepticism of everything with credulity about everything." The irony is that the very degree of submissiveness required of you to protect you is just the thing that reduces the limited life you have to the insipid minimum. And I myself feel ambivalent in this: I want you to be anything but passive, but I also want you to survive. Once, as a quite small boy, I responded to a bit of school bullying with my own specially selected chunk of iron, for which feat I was sent home with a letter, to my father's delight. The other boy bled very much from a split scalp, and I would do it again with the same accurate aim and the same saintly sense of justification. That there are degrees of fighting back it's hard to explain to an almost overwhelmed undersized boy; and how to explain it to a handicapped girl I just don't know. But teach it to you in mime I will, if I can.

Wandering again in our ozone-atmosphered

maze; but whatever I say is news to you. If you were here right now, I'd fuel up my best Dylan Thomas voice and chant to you the French ode on the steak-sauce label, making my own free-verse pauses:

> *Cette sauce de haute qualité*
> *est un mélange de fruits orientaux,*
> *d'épices et de vinaigre de malt.*
> *Elle est absolument pure*
> *et ne contient aucune matière*
>   *colorante synthétique.* . . .

Or, with almost identical results for you (that wide, complicitous grin), I'd render it in a parsonical falsetto, seeking to attain the authentic nasal vibrations that for some bizarre harmonic reason fuse treble tremolo with self-righteousness, especially (as I recall from performances I was forced to hear between babyhood and boyhood—not long) in those parsons who, at a certain crucial point, can soar to the pure soprano of a little choirboy (bereft of all fleshly timbre) and then slither down the scale back into putrid lewdness, their voices broken a second time, but this time as minds are broken, by the Ajax-cleanser radiance of a converted Adam's apple. A dying fall into *amen* as the chafed throat lowers over the gloss-linen collar, white as Charles Baudelaire's lace cuffs.

Eeeeee, you begin to plead. *More.* So off we go, in a non-Lydian mode somewhere between *hwyl* and descant: *ni aucun agent de conservation artificiel*

```
                              ciel!  Ee
                           fi       e
              a-         va    ti     ee
        cun  gent de  ser   tion ar       men.
  ni au-             con
```

Up and down, you see, like what I've just found: a

trampoliner upside-down in a newspaper picture, with a church spire in the background, and he is impaled on it right through his throat at what seems to be a height of two hundred feet, such are the accidents of press photography. Better, my girl, to be quasi-impaled on a spire than to have an eagle pecking at your liver, especially when it grows whole and edibly pulpy again each night—new every morning, like the *pâté* in the good delicatessens. Some eagles have it made and some make their own. Some, like the big brass polished eagles that hump Bibles on their backs in churches, needn't stir; but others eat blood-flavored dust, like all those eagles that André Gide wanted to commandeer when he said *il faut avoir un aigle*—you simply have to have an eagle—and you could see that he thought all worthwhile men of letters wouldn't function at all if they weren't being pecked at, not hen-pecked and therefore all goosefleshed, but eagle-chewed, whereas all those eagles ever got was livers like balloons loaded with baking powder. First catch your eagle. . . .

I sometimes, when I feel low or have what I call the coffee jitters (which don't always come from drinking my favorite imported Colombian but from another caffeine called anticipation-of-your-future), think *you* are *my* eagle. Don't lose your temper, I don't think it for long; and, anyway, you've pecked more out of your mother (there are no medals for being pecked, so hardly anybody knows) than out of me, and you are more majestic than predatory. As you see, the bile boils up and we could get damned close to quarreling, especially when I estimate the honest chances of your quelling me with a misquote from Gide written in lipstick across a two-page spread ripped out of *Elle* (or *Luie* or *El*— whatever it might be by then) and sent postage-due, incorrectly postal-coded from some college with a dragon president who yelled Hit the Road when the visiting speaker tried to bring his children for breakfast into the dining room only the morning after he'd pronounced on Diagnostic Metaphors in the haiku of Samuel Beckett. Tweeded women come and go, but only the tweed lasts. You could always wire me something lunatic:

> just discovered coffee from *qahweh* from Turk. from Arab. STOP compare *yahweh* STOP have switched to philology STOP a house not a home but a café maybe STOP leaving for Cape Wrath tonight STOP unsigned.

I am reminded—well, of two things:

> From ghoulies and ghosties and long-leggety beasties,
> And things that go bump in the night,
> Good Lord, deliver us!

And then this shameless puerile ditty from the Great Hunger:

> Honey, when you vomit,
> Save the biggest bits for me;
> I know gentility condemns it,
> But it's true econom-ee.

Between ourselves, it must be awful to be that poor, with hardly a Space Patrol sugar cigarette to your name, or even a Quiz Nougat, Raspberry Flavor, that asks you on the wrapper, "Is Ceylon in the Northern or Southern Hemisphere?" The answer, "Northern," is inside in mirror-printed capitals. That answer would have been better halfway down the nougat, but that's not how they do these things: Creem-Arrow toffee, Jelly Babies and Thirst Quencher sherbet, they all do the same. Keep you from answering.

After flying on one of those great-circle routes our eagles are coming back to us again. The message they bring, minus its claws, is that I'd be awfully glad if, one day, you didn't write a letter or send a wire, all that remote stuff, but just sauntered across the room one day with a mouthful of nougat ice cream toffee sherbet peppermint lozenges nuts garlic clove cold lamb hot radish raw cabbage cool *pâté* bananaskins Kleenex eagles' feathers and said only, "Why don't you ever shave?"

I would then use with you, happily on slide or swing seat, any oven cleanser to which I'm allergic, having had a year's dermatitis from it, when my fingers were always bleeding under and from under the Band-aids. I'd even try to relight those indoor fireworks you wanted to "wind" again as soon as they'd burned out: the charred black plume-on-wire that is the end of a sparkler; the dot of black dust that was a white pill called the North Pole and for a few seconds flared iceberg electric blue; the dry ashes, but still in coils, of Snakes in the Grass that spewed and wriggled moltenly out of a tiny stud of chemical stuck on a card; the defunct nose of the elephant that curled forward as if there were a snake charmer behind it; thinner than matchsticks, the white twig-cigarettes in the clown's mouth that puffed and puffed; the exploding tongue of another clown, the thing we lit being a short length of cap-gun ammunition pasted against his mouth; the Flashing Lighthouse that became a knot of pure light and stayed on my retina fifteen minutes after it had become a cinder.

I'd climb up the house painter's ladders with you, behind you; spring around in Hush Puppies just as if we lived in a commercial. I'd actually make you some deep-fried batter balls, which is what they threw in New Orleans to Hush the Puppies around the fried-fish stalls when they were going half mad with the aromas of fish in hot fat mixed with the aromas of the comparatively cool Gulf of Mexico. You—who take a loaf to feed the inland gulls with, who rock your head side to side like the cobra charmers of the Deccan, whom I interrupt in your non-stop vaudeville by thumping my heel on the floor (no use to call when your back is turned), whom I meet in my mind's eye at all your ages, those gone and those to come, and then find right at hand your paradoxical, jaunty self in one of your thousand roles—you, as Miss Chatterbox, I'd celebrate in one blasphemous hyperbole. *Stop evolution now,* I'd yell at your first five-word question, *it's all evolved!*

6.

Refund from Alpha 3

Play truant with you? Of course. Come, let's ride a painted elephant into the Palace of Amber; let's doss down in the bedchamber of an absentee Maharajah, play tag in the checkered courtyard where the emperor Akbar used to play chess with inert slave girls for pieces, bathe in the sun on templed beaches, or, if it's summer, let's to the hill resorts, having left behind all our dangerous drugs, live plants, gold coins, gold and silver bullion and silver-coins-not-in-current-use, at the Head Police Office in Bombay or the Talkatora Barracks in New Delhi. Two things out of three in India are called Victoria, so let's feel free to be Victorian-regal ourselves in Simla Mussoorie Nainital Darjeeling Shillong Ootacamund Kodaikanal Pachmarhi the Kulu and Kashmir Valleys and Mount Abu munching our cakes frosted with gold and silver where even the water has a bottled vintage....

Come join us on the Magnificent Holiday, that's what the hostess in her Persian-carpeted cloth-of-gold sari says in the folder. View by boat the burning and bathing ghats of the holy Ganges and the dazzling peaks of the Himalayas (Hi-MARlayas!), gape at shapes in the Phirezeshah Mehta Topiary Gardens, become fertile at the *lingam* shrine on Elephanta Island, transfer to the seaside resort of JUHU BEACH (Sun'n Sand Hotel) and Be At Leisure there before whizzing off by air to Udaipur (Lake Palace Hotel) to cruise by launch on

Pichola Lake visiting more and more palaces and, oh so soon, the Palace of Winds and by sunset the Taj Mahal after which 64,000 restaurants are named, the deserted city of Fatehpur Sikri, fragile as flaking rust, the buried city of Sarnath, the precious stone market in Kathmandu, the Buddhist temple Swayambunath two and a half thousand years old, leave by air for TIGER TOPS.

Morning drive: by Land-Rover or jeep to view crocodiles and birds!

Afternoon ride by elephant to view the jungle, and then again to Delhi to the Curio shops at Chandri Chowk, not missing Government Secretariat, Iron Pillar, Safdar Jung's (JUNG'S?) Tomb and Birla Temple. "No refund of any part of the tour price will be made to a passenger who does not take part in any excursion provided in the tour arrangements." Just so: I wonder if, together, we shouldn't seek a cosmic refund for those parts of the tour denied you without explanation, and in what currency. Why, many people would be embarrassed and downright annoyed to have you along at all, but they wouldn't quit the excursion, and so we wouldn't have it to ourselves. The only ones we have to ourselves are the private ones.

Of course, in shuffling our folders, we've flunked out in geography and garbled our itineraries, bound not to get some of our rupees back, but—*ee, ee,* you begin—don't keep *ee*ing me, I'll *give* you the brown-paper bag with the prancing elephant upon it and the split-pin fastener which encloses India Tourist Office's offset-printed slanty-columned booklet but actually looks like an air-sickness bag—I'm not the miraculous Air France memory bank, Alpha 3, the "third-generation Univac 1108 multicomputer reservations complex" which, costing the same as twenty short-haul jet-liners, can handle thirty million passengers and return information on them "in a unit of time so small relative to one second as one second is to thirty years." One hundred thousand questions an hour, and no sullen handoffs, brushoffs, like with real folks. Ask Alpha 3 any question—how many Garbo movies have been shown in flight between Kathmandu and Tiger Tops; is it cheaper by jeep than by Land-Rover when prospecting for cobras; are you expected to eat with your hands if traveling economy or tourist; are there escalators in Sarnath?—and, whether you are at a television monitor screen in London or Los Angeles, back comes the answer almost instantaneously from Alpha 3 in Paris. So don't tell me I'm not trying, I'm just not a Univac of any generation. I said we'd go someplace and someplace we'll go.

"Alpha? Testing, testing, one, t—"

"Mach two."

"Concorde? We've just built one and we'd—"

"D'accord. Cordiale!"

"Must you always exclaim? Even a Jumbo jet would ser—"

"Elephantine."

"Huh?"

"I am *not* exclaiming! Do you not recall with nostalgia the famous Air France London-Paris flight, the 'Epicurean' service? A leisurely seventy-five-minute flight with champagne and cordon-bleu cooking? And now, 7 tons of Irish salmon, 20 tons of Dakar lobsters, 6 tons of Persian caviar, 26 tons of foie gras from Hungary and the Landes, 60 tons of Colombian coffee, Chilean avocados and cherries, Kenya strawberries, Californian asparagus (all until the pick of the French crop is ready, naturally), Scotch from a special Chivas vat, all enclosed in fast elegant aluminum pencils upholstered in 8,000 yards of rich blues, old golds, and parchments (the tone, not the stuff), 8,000 yards of carpet, 90 other fabrics and third-third-of-the-century new Espace Universel seats designed following an ergonomic survey of 4,000 air travelers and—

"Ergowhat?"

"Shush, as we Univacs say; I am Alpha 3. And omega too. Ergo, shush. And in each first-class lounge original tapestries commissioned from master weavers all over the world, lightweight individual headphones allowing you a personal choice of seven music programs ranging from Beethoven to Basin Street, movie sound tracks—"

"We're sold. Now, about . . ."

And that, my girl, is how they carry on at you, these Alphas, careful never to route you over or through the war zones or where the poverty isn't at least half-picturesque or where the politics has become boorish enough to plough up the squares of a neighboring capital with tanks' treads in order to plant who knows what dismal, monolithic seed. Oh, I suppose you *could,* if you wanted it badly enough, get into these places on some sort of Emergency Package deal, but I wouldn't want to see you trying to swab the napalm off your chin with a wad of Kleenex dipped in mayonnaise, or pinching the horn-palm of a receptive leper, or smacking the turret of a Russian tank with your brand-new Slovakian umbrella. It wouldn't be the trouble of getting some of your money back, but the chore of getting yourself out. So, as for a long time now, we travel to trouble as well as to apparent idylls on our own magic staircarpet of photogravure with some of the colors coming off, which is how you prefer to travel anywhere anyway. Buckle our belts, order some fizzy *beebee,* and off we shoot in the mockup Concorde, the view from the windows and the tours on the ground nothing but picture postcards or folders at which you stare with Crusoe-Kreutznaer curiosity, calling out for scissors, drinks, ice cream, pens and paper, with all of which, as the wonders flash and ripple in our hands, I steward you toward—

Kal Bhairab, in Nepal, a dog-faced white-eyed golliwog statue with a red-hot golden crown between two sort-of baying lions, with a pink-beige temple in the offing and a well-wrapped child in a woollen ski cap, so it must be winter. Swing south here, and you at once haul out and replace your right hearing aid as if you weren't getting Beethoven or Basin Street in good tune. Down there, folks, you see two junks, they look like big maple leaves assembled from patches of ravioli-shaped sailcloth and set floating on end on hulls the shape of sewing-machine shuttles, not much moving as the Concorde flies but always with sea to spare. See now, in supersonic prying telescopic close-up, a gat-toothed young man, backed by the golden minarets of some pavilion, playing a crude stringed something or other, only his hands visible, the rest of him kept for warmth under a green sacking shawl, the bow arrested at the start of a pathetic-looking push while his feet stand on a rough mortar which is the roof of a building of not quite equal height. He lean-sits against a shallow parapet and has probably never heard of Ludwig van Beethoven or even Basin Street or you, and, if he had been born deaf etc., would have lived on deaf etc., a butt and a freak and obliged to become a mute as well. We are at present overflying a secluded promenade on a temple's top along which an elephant in a silver quilt is plodding at over a thousand feet, which is not at all a bad height for an elephant to be. The temple is on a hilltop, but we've already gone and are fanning over palms that look like enormous black false eyelashes on trunks stabbed into a deserted beach of biscuit-pale sa—

it's gone, jehosophat, oops, caramba, *floosh!*

it's those azure mountains of Japan, my that was quick, with in the violet sea between them and some down-curving carpentered bridge a half-sunk roof of something abandoned, whose terra-cotta pillars hold up a sagging slice of roof which maybe is the Japanese character for loneliness, writ large and then marooned in a reservoir, only we've no time to ponder in, we've hit the shimmering mosaics of Isfahan's Blue Mosque, a dark-blue courtyard facing the minutely scabbed stone face that's topped by a silver dome and flanked by a lighthouse whose own blue is the same as the blue of the working shirts and trousers of Frenchmen in the Midi, a luminous sun-juiced blue.

All right, you want to cut it out?—the steward saw the pink light come on as you rang *plink-plink* and here are your scissors, madam, a lovely day for cutting out blue mosques.

Oh, there? Baalbek, all steps and pillars and blocks and cylinders of stone that sit on or near green English lawns, I don't know why. You want the flight plan now? We're only here to oblige, but there isn't one: we trip at convulsive random, here today and here tomorrow, just concentrically panoramic while you wait. Los Angeles at night below us now, a shallow spill of electric lights across a mauve corrugation that is water, the windows coming ablaze in spurts and zigzags that stop short and then unvaryingly stay while the lights in another piece come on in disjointed castellation, and it's just like when I sit down to think what to tell you and there are only one or two points of light, then lights go on in all quarters and it's like electric scoreboards everywhere crammed with ever-changing information I must get to you before it's later than ever. He who quickly gives gives twice. Helen Keller said literature was her Utopia, explaining, "Here I am not disfranchised. No barrier of the senses shuts me out from the sweet, gracious discourse of my book-friends." So to postcards and folders we come: glut you with wonders, whether natural or man-made, so long as they are wonders truly, which means the same as saying anything the eye can see. Not quite, but nearly.

Without so much as asking to, you can ride the bus that goes from Jidda sixty-five miles across the Arabian desert to Mecca, the Forbidden City. Sir Richard Burton was the first European to get into it, and that was in 1853; he was disguised as an Indian. Since then, only half a dozen or so heathens have managed to do the same. Just a few years ago, three fair-haired men with cameras were stoned to death at the city's gates, and then it was found they were authentic Moslem pilgrims. But, if we could only sufficiently disguise your own blond hair, you might have better luck and, getting past the final checkpoint, cry with the pilgrims, *Labbaik, Allahumma, Labbaik!* announcing to God that you have come—or your own approximation to those sounds, with the *b*'s proving especially easy.

And now, fantastically shrugging off the oven-heat of 120° Fahrenheit, you scramble with the rest through the maze of incongruously modern houses to the Mosque of the Sanctuary, where, as tradition has it, Adam went to rest and repent after being expelled from Eden. The oldest building in the world the Moslems call it. Massive walls enclose it and Wahabi warriors with swords stand on perpetual guard. You enter, barefoot, through one of the nineteen archways and see first the Black Stone, a meteorite brought to earth by the angel Gabriel to be given to Abraham and Ishmael as the foundation stone of a new temple to be built after the Flood. None of your rocking or bird calls here, if you please; this is one of the building blocks of creation, incongruous and vast as the slab in the film called *2001, A Space Odyssey,* some stills from which excited you so much (the weightless floating, the metal ladders, and all that inside-a-plane decor). You'll need your energy anyway for the obligatory sprint, seven times over, along the Pilgrim's Way, refreshing yourself from time to time with perfumed Afghan tea or, the bitterest *beebee* of all, the milk of Turkestan. Then, to be on the safe side, plod off to the Valley of Arafat, where you have a sheep ritually butchered on your behalf, thus adding your two cents' worth to the abattoir reek of the valley where even the pilgrims topple and die of heat stroke, their bodies often being left there until the next day to bulge and bloat.

Poo! you shriek, and are understandably relieved to move on in order to perform the last rite of slinging stones at the Three Pillars of Satan, monuments marking the spot where Satan three times appeared, three times tempted the son of Abraham, and was thrice stoned. It is just as well you should go now; these Moslems don't take kindly to small pilgrims answering the *muezzin* back in a shrill call so like his own that the faithful become confused, then threaten you with stones, while the *muezzin* himself comes wheezing down from his minaret only to burn his hand accidentally on the Black Stone as it waxes radioactive again, melting the swords of the Wahabi guards and giving off a fierce pulsating violet light that metamorphoses you into Eve as, with fazer gun in your fist, you depart through the same archway you entered by, a touch of punctilious autism which is really sheer bravado as well. An E-type Jaguar sleek but not gaudy rushes you back to Jidda, to the new airport on the Red Sea coast, and your private Concorde has you safely in the smoke clouds over Popocatepetl, the volcano southeast of Mexico City, long before, on the *muezzin*'s command, thousands of pilgrims fling themselves upon and round the death-emitting Black Stone to shield the Forbidden City from its rays.

No time at all, and you are negotiating the 248 steps which lead to the top of the main pyramid of thousand-year-old San Juan Teotihuacán, your mini-skirt rolled up high, a bunch of gladioli in one hand, a big black doorstep of ice cream in the other, no sign of your fazer. Then you descend, go out dressed in *mariachi* costume—fancy velvet jacket, tight pants, high-heeled boots and a sombrero—to eat tamales, dare the Aztec Gallop or Montezuma's Revenge to plague you. You beckon the trumpets of the little band to close in on your right ear and order tequila all round, from Mecca to Mexico in a wink, the perfect escape.

Where to now? Which places forbidden or open? The air-conditioned out-of-doors in the Houston Astropark where Mark Hofheinz, the electronic Barnum who declares "all the money I ever made was by hypothecating my previous accumulations," first created the perfect climate within the Astrodome and then decided to change the outside climate too. Will you ride his choo-choo that has a cow catcher out front? Will you steer one of his kiddie cars that advance at about the same two miles an hour as that two-thousand-ton contraption on caterpillar tracks which picks up a moon rocket bodily at Cape Kennedy and carries it upright the three and a half miles to the firing pad in just over a hundred minutes?

Or will you visit the site, at Ardis in Turkey, of King Croesus' gold refinery, go rummage in his sixth century B.C. workshop among the bits of gold, the remnants of crucibles, blow-pipes, nozzles, and more than three hundred clay basins? It was Harvard University that found it, so maybe we should apply to Cambridge, Mass., for permission to go. Or will you visit the British factory in St. Albans that manufactures pasta for Italy and, by much the same process, used to produce straw for hats? And perversely order a hat made from semolina and durum wheat? Or a spaghetti cape?

Or will you zoom off into a future which, yours anyway, brings shopping by picture telephone with speech being sent as light down a glass line, television sets as thin as dinner plates, microwave cookery that readies your steaks in one minute, lawns that grow to the desired height and then stop, programmed and undriven electric polythene cars, hovertrains that go at half the speed of sound on a cushion of air, titanium airliners fueled with hydrogen that exceed three thousand miles an hour, wines from new vineyards such as Château Woomera and Châteauneuf du Module, bottled suntans that never fade and vibro-hammocks in the garden, transparent water pipes and self-cleansing baths?

No future? *Few-cha?* Your wish is my command as we zero in on Nathan S. Jacobson's CAESAR'S PALACE hotel set in imported-cypress gardens where the Venus de Milo partners the Canova and Medici Venuses, all in marble substitute and built, "built," *built*—Las Vegas built, this is Vegas not Ancient or Renaissance anything—and smirking Roman centurions take our flimsy, ill-traveling bags away on a litter past a Nero's Nook full of latterday Messalinas in peacock-feathered togas and up we go to the sumptuous ersatz-marble bath whose taps are crystal bulbs so pure-looking we want to read the diminished future into them before bathing and then launching ourselves into the dazzling, sunlorn town to view the Leaning Tower of Pizza, all cherry fluorescence, and the Biggest Beer in the World outpouring itself into a colossal glass frosted with archangels' breath, and so to no bed but a whole night wrestling with one-armed bandits you need two arms to shift at all, our very early breakfast taken at Mr. Sy's souvenir and gift shop, which is also the U.S. Post Office, and then we retreat only just before 90 degrees F. becomes 100 degrees F. But already a pastel telephone is paging us, it's time to rise and start another day. . . .

Oh, you'd rather be a lunarnaut, would you? Or

travel to Florida to test the acoustics of the Vertical Assembly Building, which has a 470-foot door that takes an hour to open and is so high it has to be airconditioned to prevent clouds from forming in the ceiling (as befits the Biggest Building in the World, sufficient to contain two Buckingham Palaces). Or shall we be ultra-cautious and, in scarlet chiffon scarves and goggles and leather helmets, sit quietly on our own grass in our replica of an ancient Fokker monoplane which, if it took off, could fly for a full hour on seven gallons of eighty-octane fuel? I don't blame you for *ee*ing me time and again; everything's out there waiting for us to tackle it, except, with us, getting ready's almost all the doing. Our anti-handicaps are symbolic. *Votre oeil émerveillé,* as the Saint-Malo civic scroll puts it, *s'étonnera:* eye-stunned from staring upon marvels, you'll dream unsurpassable dreams no satellite can ever transmit. When you speak, you move the whole front of your face, giving each sound its labial, muscular, breathing maximum; you do not waste what is rare and you find what is marvelous in what is commonplace, teamed up with and part of and taking for granted all things bizarre or exotic.

The outstanding thing about tomorrow, I can now reveal, is that you will be seven years old. You don't know what a year is and so won't find anything outstanding in this occasion unless we make a splash. A large cake with candles you'll more or less count and then extinguish with a giant puff, a replacement for the VC-10 airliner whose tail is awry and Scotch-taped together, the piccolo you howled for, a plastic garden swing and a slide made in Japan, a pair of snow-white soft mittens, yet another jigsaw puzzle—these and some routine items that you'd get in any case (poster colors, crayons, new painting book) will help to make the day, especially on top of the little party you'll be having at school—an exceptionally festive affair in itself because your birthday also happens to be the last day of school before half term. I only hope you won't think deprivation always accompanies largess in that your birthday somehow inaugurates No School for ten days. You very easily construe coincidences, the irony being that you have enough vocabulary to obtain basic facts from us but explanations hardly at all. And there's something else: Saturday and Sunday, the days after your birthday, you'd have off anyway, so the puzzlement will come on Monday morning when, like someone putting one of those Latin questions which anticipate the answer *yes*, you'll ask about *kool* with your usual premature celebratory grin. Which will dwindle as you realize you are entering another of those uncertain periods which begin and end you know not why and deny you your favorite daytime activity, and then, just when you've reconciled yourself to all the resuscitated pastimes of weekday life at home, pluck you out to school again after an interim for which you have no word but which you accept—with the same stoical skepticism with which you accept so much—as yet another inscrutable movement of Environment against you.

Sometimes, thus baffled, you spend days in reserved offendedness, trying perhaps to detect the pattern, the purpose, the profit, even going so far as to extrapolate in your non-verbal way, although you don't really know where one pattern begins and its neighbor ends or why some days resemble one another and others don't. There is a void everywhere just beyond the edge of what you find familiar, and essentially you are living in a dark through which others shepherd you and in which they illuminate precious zones like the tops of certain mushrooms in a thousand-acre forest. Yours is the most precarious existentialism of all; or, to put it in words that I'm sure you'd prefer, you are, although inventive and energetic and quick on the uptake, one of the most dependent people I know. Which makes you one of the most trusting creatures in Creation.

But—the brighter side—I'm glad you aren't one of those children who, at half term or term's end, see all the cases and hampers in the school's main hall, packed by house mothers for parents to collect; all except their own. These children either stay or are billeted out, and at first they scream. Even you, a day girl, looked mortified on the afternoon before your first half-term holiday began; you saw all the baggage, the cars and taxis and buses, and concluded, I think, school was over for life and had been just another of those temporary experiences you'd never become inured to, leaving your life as they did without plan or dimension, scope or even fabric. Too, none of the baggage belonged to you, so you assumed that here, by some extra twist of the knife, you'd been subjected to the refined insult of dispossession before having even owned. You'd been to *kool*, it was over forever, and no one had even given you a bag to go away with. The look on your face evoked the horrors of another scene: persecution, deportation, the refusal of their own identities to people helpless, submissive, willing to be sent anywhere so long as it was soon over with, victims—very literally—of biological inheritance. Jews and gypsies; cattle trucks and open wagons; the holds of slave ships; and when I used that phrase "portable ghetto" a little while back, I meant just that. Forgive us our memberships as we forgive those who blackball us.

And now your birthday, this eighteenth of October, has begun, in the first week of the Mexican Olympic Games. You have gone off to school brandishing my sketch of a birthday cake and shouting *zeven*. Your birthday cards are lined up on the mantel like the Wahabi guards at Mecca, and there is even one that came in a package sent to you by Alitalia, a publicity gimmick which nonetheless greets you with "OPEN

YOUR GATEWAY" on the front and clinches matters on the back with "TO THE WORLD," the one showing a country cottage through a close-up of a wicket gate, the other an eclectic landscape with Leaning Tower of Pisa, one kangaroo and several minarets, a butterfly and a stylized lion, all shone over by a rosebud-mouthed psychedelic sun with a spectrum halo. Inside —what could be better?—there's a rear view of a parked Alitalia Caravelle with its boarding ramp down. All right, this fortuitous bonus has stolen our thunder, but you have at least, while cramming egg into your incessantly moving mouth with your inferior hand (the right), domesticated the offering with a brilliant, nervous-lined sketch of your mother standing behind what looks like a horizontal-barred gate.

Elsewhere—"else" being too weak a word to convey all that distance and all the otherness of Mexico—the Poles in the Olympic village have dropped water-loaded plastic bags on the Guineans' heads and the Guineans have slung stones and slates at the Poles, an *affaire* you would impartially have enjoyed. One Olympic present I would have liked to give you, but you aren't ready yet for such inspiriting identifications-with: I mean watching, while understanding all that goes into it, the performance of V. Skomarokhov, the "deaf-mute" Russian who came fifth in the four-hundred-meter hurdles and wasn't in the least put out by two false starts. That run of his was worth a ton of the world's rough ridicule and seven whole, although fragmentary, years of apartness. I know, I know, we've an overdeveloped response to the handicapped who excel, as well as to those who don't—Olympic runner or your tiny friend at school who has fewer words than you—but such are the hyperboles of care. Let's leave it at that; I promise not to bug you again with V. Skomarokhov, Lon Chaney, Ludwig van Beethoven, Frederick Delius, Helen Keller, Goya, Lenny, and

Poor Tom, or to begin producing such other trump cards as Ronsard, Du Bellay, Thomas Edison, Marie de Bashkirtseff, and Charles Maurras, all deaf, or David Wright, the deaf poet, whose stunning autobiography I've just reviewed, or Jack Clemo, the poet who is deaf-blind. Everything in your own time, just providing you'll let us drive you a little and give us the right to pester you later—after later—with an absolute gallery of true Olympians who've competed against something even more crippling, and more permanently so, than the thin air of Mexico City. And have won. You yourself begin with an almost satirical view of humanity and so won't take competition too seriously, aware before beginning of the variety of human wishes.

The other morning when you arrived at school, there was a whole cohort of people assembled on the steps: students, come to spend a day either observing or teaching. Without seeming to observe *them* (which maybe taught them something), you assimilated the throng's appearance, especially the nun and the colored woman, whom you have identified for all time as the penguin and the golly. See, I knew you knew "penguin," but I forgot to include it in your list of words. Going back to rectify the omission would be to cheat a little, and, anyway, informality not perfection is the mode of our rambling letter.

Crackle, *wham,* a jet has just gone over, taking off in the opposite direction from usual; the wind has changed for your birthday. I even think you might have heard that big fart from the afterburners; maybe Alitalia was up there, greeting you again, and I can't check because I've no timetable and I didn't see the plane even though I got to the window in two strides. But perhaps you wouldn't have noticed, or attended, anyway; as with the penguin and the golly, when you are intent, you have a boorish dimissory way with you that simply says *You are not there,* which is how you reach your destinations while marching through this baroque shambles of a house or through Saturday crowds on your way to the escalator. What, I wonder, could ever detain you? not even planes or umbrellas in shopwindows, not even something as outlandish as the 4½-inch nose of Bell, who did the engravings for the first *Encyclopaedia Britannica* and who, embarrassed, would hide it in his handkerchief or even disguise it with a more pleasingly shaped artificial nose. What does detain you, with an almost perfect record, is the play park when you are returning from an outing: even in the dark, whether or not it is also freezing or the rain is coming down in thick rods, you have to do the ritual slide, the ritual swing, your bottom and feet thumping into the snow or the mud, and let the world think what it will on its way to hell.

Slam-zhoor, another jet goes over. Sometimes this house is like the bridge of an aircraft carrier and I can half persuade myself I hear the tin voice that runs it all: "Launch jets," nasal and impersonal and then the empty clank, more appropriate to belowdecks than to the bridge, after the plane has blazed away. *Why mention the bridge at all then?* I hear you say, holding up between finger and thumb a bit of my prose with that sardonic preciosity of yours. You similarly held up a nail-shaped bit of plastic you'd found on the carpet, valuing it against the light and then checking it against our fingers to see who might have lost an entire nail. Then you wanted to extend your inspection to feet. . . .

All actions, even taking our shoes and socks off, even telling you what you never understand, can help you to exist that little bit more, so that you bulk a bit larger in this world; not in the specialized enclaves of school or clinic, but in the so-called marketplace where you may, to the uninitiated, seem incongruous, like the deaf girl I read about who whenever out in public recited her lines from the school nativity play, in which, as a cow, she announced, "I am a cow. My milk shall nourish the mother this day, whose Child shall nourish mankind always." Which is language such as you have never dreamed of, but animated all the same by the same extraordinary confidence as your explaining to strangers who you are by pointing to your chest and shouting your name.

This demand for recognition as *you* is something not to waste; something that isn't wasted, for instance (if I may go afield again), in the Camphill Village Communities for mentally handicapped adults, where each person has a special thing (the positive which the negative of his handicap generates) to give to another: the mongols, affectionate and euphoric folk always, are ideally equipped to befriend the psychotics, and the autistic often respond profoundly to those whose handicap is physical as well. Kindliness, tolerance thrive, and the dark or night side of human nature shows surprisingly little—which is reassuring to one who knows that deaf children, because they are deaf, aren't "good" any more than, say, hearing parents are because they can hear. It is good to know that, in no matter how limited a setting, handicaps can be put to use. Thus, in the case of the community called Botton Village, we find Roger and Simon, both of them deaf and psychotic; but Simon helps Roger at bedtime and has in general helped to improve his attitude to people around him; Roger, it also happens, is almost blind and is paralyzed down his left side. Here before me, in fact, is a photograph of Simon in the act of washing Roger's feet: Simon seems to be grinning as he holds up to the light something, maybe a talent he had lost, he's found between Roger's toes, and Roger is watching him as he sits in his chair, his feet set relaxedly in the plastic bowl on the floor. Or take Ben, the blind baker of the village's bread, who calls his oven "Sarah"—"the hottest girl in

Botton." Or Ruth, deaf and dumb and psychotic, who engraves glass with uncanny skill.

They all work to keep the village going and so win a role, an identity, a duty of care, and in a milieu which, although an enclave, is a functioning, unbigoted, people-fulfilling society safer than the United States, less class-conscious than Britain at large, less finicky than France; tighter than a *polis,* more human than an institution, more chivalrous than any suburb. It's a microcosm in which discovery, not prescription, counts; in which the people explore and invent in a way not much different, in principle, from that recommended by Alain Robbe-Grillet for the "new novelist," or, if we can get very personal (as when we say *seven,* at which you blush), from what Saul Maloff, commenting in *Newsweek* on the trial-run essay I wrote about you, correctly identified as the process by which your "strange and beautiful presence in the world" compelled me "to rethink and resee [my] own relation to the natural and human universe."

So let's give a quick, not very orthodox salute to those people on the outside who understand (as well as to those on the inside who've come, however limitedly, into their own). What a pleasure it is to note that Viennese refugees in 1939 took the trouble to pioneer a movement to assist the handicapped and so very practically implement the teachings of another Austrian, Rudolf Steiner. About what goes on when you're out and about, we'll say more later; it's your birthday and I was forgetting the special fanfare I had in mind, something to get your mind off my own intermittent ponderosity and on to the marzipan pageant surrounding you whether you notice it or not. Can you count all the way through October? Well, you were born on the day between the anniversary of Walgren's Super Value Days and the anniversary of the Medina Temple Oriental Pageant (so my *Esquire* Guide to Drink says);

in fact, you were born on Alaska Day, and I wonder why they bother to celebrate that or any of those other supererogated non-occasions. Next year we'll send a cable to Alaska, filling up their calendar at last.

That, surely, would improve on even Alitalia's brilliant timing or any open "new gateway to the world." Until I knew I had to bring the world to you, I don't think I knew or saw the world at all; and I don't mean just the handicapped of all sorts and conditions, such as your classmates who came to your last birthday's party and pummeled, romped, and Sherman-tanked their way all over the house and the garden and your toys while you, immaculately adaptable, stood by smiling the smile of the giving and forgiving hostess as they took over the toys of your entire lifetime in a boy-dominated orgy of dangling, whistling earpieces, cream-plastered faces and paws, upturned paper cups, sat-on éclairs, catapulted spoonfuls of jelly, spurned sensible sandwiches, purloined lollipops, crashed jetliners, chewed candles, and miniature umbrellas all in the up position, the tiniest boy howling in a private trauma and the others whoopeeing and sirening fit to dement the damned, with the one other girl meekly talking to herself under your best Tokyo parasol while I, ringmaster-clown, studied my *dramatis personae* and asked you who was who only to get a contemptuous leer in return, and your mother wiped bottoms, blotted up pools and in between times plugged the ceaselessly enunciating pairs of jaws with cake.

At the end, after they had all been worked into the wrong coats, some of the boys apparently having come in coats that existed no more or had mutated beyond recognition in the course of two hours, you took one look at the battlefield and at once headed for the bathroom, half in shock, half exhausted with delight at having carried without mishap through the entire party your big model bath. Most of the Polaroid pictures of that event survive, and you study them from time to time with the air of a pilot who, having been shot down, watches someone's wing-camera pictures of his fall, knowing he'd survived but paying especial attention to the frames immediately before he bailed out.

This time, however, we plan a mild celebration at which you will be able to queen it semi-sedately, play with your presents before they get smashed, and have no competition at all for the toilet. Some paper hats and crackers will provide a flimsy pageantry while I, having read some works I wish I could forget, hear time's winged Wordsworth at my back, resist the lines but can't dismiss them; so I let them through from "We Are Seven":

> A simple child,
> That lightly draws its breath,
> And feels its life in every limb....

You blew out the candles in two goes; you ate the icing and ignored the cake, reserving your most meticulous attention for the tiny ballerina we'd set in place right by your name in the green ice writing. You made me blow up every balloon, taxi and make take off the gleaming white VC-10 (HEAR ITS AIRFIELD JET WHINE! shouted the box lid), play the piccolo right into your ear (although I couldn't get anywhere near the two tunes supplied—"Baa! Baa! Black Sheep" and "Jingle Bells"), don the green devil mask and chase you, and even show you how to open one Sava Ham packed by 29 November Meat Industry, Subotica, Yugoslavia, and exported by Koproduct Novi Sad (which would have been exotic enough on its own without the marshmallows you combined it with).

We worked the knots out of our systems, all of us, and you insisted on chanting down the piccolo instead of blowing into it and you made us all wear paper hats

Words for a Deaf Daughter 161

and you let your own slide down over your eyes and didn't even adjust it, taking the party half blind, then, and quite unable to separate all the *sevens* we said from your memory of last Christmas. Upon seeing the stack of presents with the fanged mask on top you whipped round at once to the corner where, if it had been Christmas really, the tree would have been. But no tree; what event was this?

Nothing, I suppose, stranger than some of the items in a list that has just come to my hand of the universe's bizarreries being teased out by sly researchers who, by now, know all about Egg Weight, Shell Thickness, and Blood Spot Incidence in Solar and Windowless Poultry Houses; the Embrittlement of Babbitt-Bronze Bonds; the Influence of Forming Die on Hay Wafer Stability; Mushroom Shrinkage During Processing; the Response of the Crayfish *Cambarus b. bartoni* to a Vibratory Stimulus; Consumer Preference for Christmas Trees in a Mature Market Area; New Gamma Rays from Au 197; Honeybee Foraging on Buckwheat and the Relationship to Yield of Grain; the Rate of Dissipation of Eddy Energy in the Lowest 100 Metres of the Atmosphere; Plastic Buckling of Rib Cored Cylindrical Sandwich Shells Subjected to Hydrostatic Pressure; The Decay of Xe 137; Birdsfoot Trefoil and Cottontail Rabbits—Consumptive and Reproductive Effects; the Effect of Leading Edge Blowing on the Lift Characteristics of a Low Aspect Ratio Delta Wing; Virginal and Non-Virginal College Girls Compared; the Modigliani-Brumberg-Ando Consumption Function; Genetic Variation of White Pine Characteristics Related to Weevil Attack; Sour Cherry Necrotic Ringspot and Clover Mosaic Viruses; the Effect of Newcastle Disease Virus Infection on Succinate Respiration in Primary Cultured Chick Embryo Cells; Haematology of the Guinea Pig at Varying Ascorbic Acid Levels; Underwater Flutter; and even Relationships

Among Abnormal Auditory Adaption, Differential Intensity Sensitivity, and Performance with a Hearing Aid.

Sic! You are a member of a stunning universe, so much of which is closed to you, much more, even, than is closed to the vast majority of us.

Let us, therefore, in compensation to you, thicken up your birthday, shower you with astounding gifts, from the entire surface of the Velodrome in Mexico City (a tough African wood called "Douzzie Afzelia"), where cycling events are held, to Emperor Frederick II's treatise, *The Art of Falconry,* dating from around 1260, with over nine hundred cameos of birds, animals, cities, and landscapes, and currently in the Vatican Library; from a wall one hundred yards long and twenty high, on which we'll write a soap mural with cans of instant lather, to Ludwig van Beethoven's three legless pianos; from here always to there; from the Nile Valley, where UNESCO has had the colossal faces of Rameses II and Nefertiti sawn out of the cliff face and raised two hundred feet clear of what has now become the Aswan High Dam, to Brussels, for the Jeux sans Frontières in which teams from half a dozen nations do pillow fights on greasy poles, play one-a-side soccer with five sets of goalposts and fifty balls, and ride bicycles in big revolving drums; or from Texas, where you could go to inspect Haroldson Lafayette Hunt, who reputedly makes $200,000 a day and carries his lunch to work in a brown-paper bag and has neither Cadillac nor chauffeur, to somewhere south of Panama where a warm current called El Niño (it also is "a child" that arrives around Christmas) invades the region of the Humboldt cold-water current and so muddles the marine life there that, from exposure to the unnaturally high concentration in the water of hydrogen sulphide, the lead in the paint on the bottoms of ships changes into lead sulphide and the hulls turn black in Callao harbor, the work, they say in those parts, of the "Callao painter."

Or, for kicks, if you will, escape from Cuba to Florida by wave hopping in an ancient crop-dusting biplane thick with poisonous chemical or, because Niolai Gogol interrupted *Dead Souls* to sing its praises in print, take the *troika* on any crisp and even winter's night. Whatever you choose to accept or to do on any of your sturdy birthdays, and whether or not on one of them, like a slow genius, you suddenly come out with a long sentence after having said virtually nothing in all the years up to then, your battle hymn shall begin and end, *l'anarchie c'est moi,* with many happy returns.

7.

The Pink Forest Canal Society

You know how life is: right in the middle of writing a letter you have to go off and give a lecture, halfway through which you get an idea you want to maneuver into the latest chapter of whatever it is you're hoping is going to be a book, but which you've put on one side in order to read a book that has just come for review, which is also why you never catch up on all those bumper issues of the *Times Literary Supplement*, whose clock at the head of the editorial column is stuck always at half past four, the very time at which, over a cup of sweet-and-brown sergeant-major tea, you seem to remember having promised an essay whose topic you haven't yet decided—it's a bit dazing, with all these disconnected intermittences that have to be fitted into a day-sandwich you can hold and eat.

I've been reading, on a sidetrack, a book called *All The Little Animals,* by Walker Hamilton, a bare and succinct novel about the mind and adventures of a mentally slow thirty-one-year-old called Bobby Platt who has run away from a crass, punitive stepfather he calls "The Fat" and has taken up with one Mr. Summers, a bank manager turned bum, whose entire vocation is to scour the highways for run-over animals and to bury them. "People can bury each other, boy," Mr.

Summers tells him, "but the animals have to be helped." Bobby eventually succeeds him as traveling sexton to the slaughtered, but not before the two of them have disastrously attempted to slaughter The Fat himself. What I especially liked was the book's multitude of quiet visits with the flora and fauna of the Cornish countryside, where Mr. Summers and Bobby live together in a hut and go in for a good deal of drop-out philosophizing. Mr. Summers when he sees a cow sees it as "life in the shape of a cow," whereas Bobby—as much a natural naturalist as you—makes a virtue of not interpreting—as when, nose to the ground, he studies "the tiny things in the grass roots . . . as if I were small like the things I was watching." Such a simplicity of mind fascinates me: the so-called human picture isn't complete without it and human humility cannot be said to have begun until the mind, so-called, has accepted it. Walker Hamilton takes a sizable chance: confined within Bobby's rudimentary idiom, he can't rhetoricize the intricacies of Bobby's private psychodrama, but he wins out by exemplifying so precisely what Bobby sees that we learn from Bobby what Bobby cannot teach.

How, indeed, if at all, can the life of you handicapped people be put into words? Presumably you have special aptitudes that to some extent compensate for what you are short of: say, a non-verbal although perhaps intricate intimacy with animals or plants (Bobby-like) or, by the same token, with things man-made that most people in their full-facultied haste ignore or overlook—the texture of a blanket, the taste of a spoon. Attentiveness for its own sake could well be what the mentally handicapped person has as his own special gift. Intent not on reporting what he perceives but on perceiving itself, he comes closer perhaps than so-called competent people to seeing infinity in a grain of sand (although he won't think of it in that way). He might even see the *finiteness* of a grain of sand, thus heeding its excellence within its limitations.

For what it is worth, the opinion of the president of the Royal Academy is that some handicapped children "seem to have a supersensitivity, which suggests that there are certain sorts of judgment which lie outside the ordinary process of reasoned thought." Impressed by what he saw at two exhibitions of paintings by handicapped children, he told the Invalid Children's Aid Association, "I just wonder if research into the relationship of sensitivity and intelligence, perhaps through the work of these children, might not lead to a new and more realistic conception of what IQ really is. . . . Our estimation of the IQ is a very limited one, and it seems that the qualities of intelligence and judgment are left out." Walker Hamilton and President Sir Thomas Monnington, and I, seem to be at the point of abandoning Ptolemy for Copernicus, so to speak, and I just wonder if it isn't possible to get beyond even Copernicus. . . .

You, of course, are just the sort of person to tell me I'm thinking wishfully. It's hard to say, especially as, nowadays, there is developing a certain weariness with intelligence itself, with the primacy accorded to it by so many sectors of our zooming, blundering, clever civilization. We have already been instructed by our teenagers that "smartness," like ambitiousness or wealth, has little to do with "soul"; and from that lesson it isn't a far reach to find, somewhere between flower power and *satori,* a place for the mentally hindered. Awareness of, and reverence for, life seem to have ousted the old power tool of reason that brilliantly explained what awe could not. Enthusiasm—which is Greek for being possessed by a god—is back in vogue again. The mind has been telling itself to "expand" beyond all the resources of reason. In fact, all that is missing is for someone to rediscover the word *idiot* (a word smeared with hurt and cant) and remind us that it is the Greek for "a private person." Mock as people may, like the Bobby mockers in the novel, brains only get us very far—far enough to see something always farther, today's marvel being tomorrow's cliché, the future being so old-fashioned; whereas the gestures of slower minds are very often sufficient to themselves, each being equivalent to any one of the others and intended not to explain but to regard. True, if you like, to life, to the unique something between see-er and seen. To "tell it like it is" is virtually impossible, for any complete account of anything—anyone—would have to include what you yourself see anything—anyone—as; and that we don't know.

Such an observation as I've just made lodges in the mind as a challenge, surely, construable as an affront or a bad joke only by those who unwittingly prove time and again that the biggest handicap of all is to be mentally competent without being spiritually awake. After all, it's the majority of the non-handicapped (*soi-disant*) who want to shut away the handicapped, not the handicapped who want to shut *them* away. I have concluded from the behavior of all save the handicapped, the most intelligent, and the most compassionate, that man's sanity (again so-called) and his putative good will are precarious little sprouts demanding constant sheltering—or, as the physician and psychiatrist R. D. Laing puts it—that "the condition of being out of one's mind is the condition of *normal* man. Normal men have killed perhaps 100,000,000 of their fellowmen in the last fifty years." Hence the normality which, frowning at you and your exhilarated birdcalls, reinforces its own terror by wanting to have you locked away as its own proxy. As John Heywood says in his *Proverbes,* the earliest collection of English colloquial sayings, "Who is so deafe or so blinde as is hee/That wilfully will neither heare nor see?" The mind that would keep company with you must be big enough to make itself limp a little; in so doing, it might notice things it might otherwise have missed.

Yes, you'll say, but you've been lumping together all the handicaps in Creation: some, like blindness, are almost respectable, but no one has any respect for—or patience with—the deaf. Ear trumpets provoke grins, but white canes don't. Why, even Helen Keller—who once was like an unruly young animal but eventually rode and swam and truly enjoyed flying—wrote that "The problems of deafness are deeper and more complex, if not more important than those of blindness." And she was in a very privileged position to comment from. I agree with you, but it is extremely hard to translate the idiom of adjustment to one handicap into the idiom of adjustment to another: the parent of a deaf child will always involuntarily regard the blind, the spastic, the cerebral-palsied, the mongol, the autistic, as also in some way deaf. But it's better to give the wrong damn than give no damn at all, better to talk in Latin in Italy than to pretend the Romance languages don't exist.

Of all things, a walking example has just been at the door, bearing a "stand-pipe" from something called the "Pink Forest Canal Society," and we conversed briefly in mutual incomprehension, he having assumed I would know what to do with such a pipe, I marveling at the bizarre name of something that maybe doesn't even exist. We might have come from different planets—you just can't *explain* the Pink Forest Canal Society; but at least the English language helped us to establish that we couldn't enlighten each other. I am content, have to be content, to presume every handicap brings with it some ineffable virtue and to guess at the ineffable in other handicaps on the strength of the ineffable in yours, which I can guess about at first hand.

Guessing: Helen Keller kept all kinds of people guessing and many times during her life was examined to see if she possessed abnormal faculties; but all the experts agreed that she was simply making remarkable use of such faculties as she did possess. But I wonder how well equipped medical science is to establish the existence of faculties out of the ordinary. Over three decades ago the neurologist Sir Charles Sherrington decided that physics and chemistry couldn't account for mind, and in 1963 the brain specialist Sir John Eccles contended in his Eddington Memorial Lecture that "the prime reality of my experiencing self cannot with propriety be identified with brains, neurones, nerve impulses or spatial-temporal patterns of impulses." The brain doesn't generate consciousness, *is* not consciousness; and a nerve cell doesn't differ in any essential way from a muscle cell—or so it was decided at the 1966 International Symposium on Brain and Consciousness. Couldn't we say that the brain is an organ of limitation which, while channeling attention or attentiveness, cannot entirely censor the mind's subliminal activities?

I'm saying it anyway in befuddled recognition of the fact that we understand the physical world itself very little and cannot adequately describe experience. Why, it's no heresy these days to say that all science offers us is models and that we have every reason to try and develop a mathematics of qualities. What exactly your conscious and unconscious experiences are like I do not know: you are, if not quite a law unto yourself, at least your own Xanadu, your own palace of varieties, which is looking on the bright side, or—looking on the other, which it is painful to do—your own wasteland, your own lunar surface. The why of your condition no one has told us; that it isn't similar to ours is evident; and whether or not we know about them, I hope you have some compensations and it is these which make you smile so much and which genially populate the vacancy into which you sometimes stare even now.

Over the long haul there's a gain of sorts: we give you all the ordinary things, treat you as far as possible like an ordinary girl, but also—if this isn't too wishfully invasive—feed to you the results of our own guessings, our own discoveries and *trouvailles*. Having been obliged to develop some extraordinary mental attitudes in order to traffic with you at all, we may be finding in that necessity exactly the virtues you can devour. And even if you don't apprehend our actions— drawings, mimes, games, and rituals—in the way we think you do, you are at least aware of our activity on your behalf: these things are being done *for you*. On a more prosaic level, it heartens us to know that completely institutionalized children come more slowly to language than children who, like you, have a daily life in two worlds. Matthew Arnold somewhere defined this kind of faith as a constant effort which, even if it failed in its primary purpose, nonetheless kept alive a needed attitude. So we try like mad to maximize whatever you have, which is like fitting a hearing aid to your whole life.

Getting to Atlantis would be one way of symbolizing it, and getting there is hard, but not as hard as if we thought getting there impossible. This is why we stick big cards on everything so you'll come to know what things are called (thus tricking you into the habit of reading) and why, also, we show you the latest as well as the most ancient painted and sculptured things (for these are indeed the voices to reach you in your profoundest silence). Your world we read as open-ended and you have made our own the same. Of the materials and the time consumed let's not even think; there is always an advance going on: you change and change and change, outstripping these words even as I set them down.

What? You haven't noticed? I'll tell you, fixing you with my Ancient Mariner's eye. Since I began this writing, you've regained one word you lost for two years (*mower,* which shaves the lawn); you've learned to say *thumb* with triumphant precision and *bubbie* (which makes the bubbles in your bathwater). And you double *mirroe,* which is not mirror only but photograph, to be uttered while squinting up your left eye behind the left fist you've screwed up into a makeshift view finder. The first time you said it (in the imperative, as always), we thought you wanted a mirror, but you screamed and screamed as we assembled all the mirrors there were (Is it *this* one she wants?), and that went on for two hours. Then those feebly construing and frantically guessing adults fished out a camera from its secret place and you smiled, jerked the tears off your face, and said *mirroe* very gently. Then we photographed you while you exultantly murmured the word you'd taught us. The logic of your semantics is visual, and you have made our own reasoning visible to us.

Too, you have begun quite spontaneously to kiss, which you do with a prim, slow-motion graveness, and to narrow your eyes while walking forward in smiling bemusement. Having sympathy to spare, you exclaim *Ah!* if we so much as touch our faces, trunks, or limbs, and you have taken to cooling your ravioli with milk. You now have other dances than your habitual rocking stamp and you increasingly clap yourself like a Russian. Best of all, you now consistently recognize and utter a dozen written words, and, one day, when you thought I wasn't noticing, you wrote your name in slurred big letters on a piece of paper and Scotch-taped it to the front of the back of your chair at the table. Having on that day sat in it without your permission, I took the hint, am still taking it.

Watching all this happen has been a bit like seeing at Passchendaele the hundredweight of metal that rises to the surface of the soil each day after rain, except that we don't even know what is buried, so anything—a fiber pen big as a Cape Kennedy rocket, the Queen of Hearts, a crystallized rainbow made of sugar—could come looming up. Even the president of the Pink Forest Canal Society, come to explain to us at long last.

You, with what aptitudes you have and with that jaunty interfering temperament of yours, have persisted. We, evolving a technique as we went along, have persisted too. And school (which the other day sent a note to say you had performed "beautifully" when taking an audiogram) has converted you into a social creature, has in fact given you a social consummation you must have devoutly wished for for years. I try to keep up with the flood of periodicals, pamphlets, and reports devoted to the plight of children handicapped like, less than, more than, you; and so I know something about flashing clocks, volume-control handsets for telephones, BBC television play synopses for the deaf, the Warren Wearable Walk-Away Units, the vibrating pillow that wakes you up and the torchlike apparatus being designed for deaf-blind children, as well as the manual-versus-oral teaching controversy, the Helen Keller Home in Tel Aviv, the clinic for deaf children founded at the University of Southern California by Mr. and Mrs. Spencer Tracy (whose son John was born deaf), the Alexander Graham Bell Award given to Lyndon Baines Johnson in 1967 "for Distinguished Service for the Deaf" and the Royal National Institute for the Deaf's bronze statuette for the Best TV Speaker of the Year.

I succumb to an anxious voracity:

the deaf of this world outnumber the combined populations of Britain, France, and Germany;

most of the research now going on is concerned with conductive deafness as distinguished from the perceptive kind (sensorineural hearing loss or *nerve* deafness), but I know that, whereas the middle ear is mechanics and engineering, the inner ear is electronics, with the cochlea functioning as an almost unthinkably complex and miniaturized telephone exchange with twenty thousand "lines." . . . One square centimeter houses equipment equivalent to that contained in one million cubic feet of a big urban exchange;

in 1968 and 1969 Congress passed two acts designed to aid handicapped children, and the appropriation works out to forty cents per child in the nation;

the Federal Bureau of Education for the Handicapped estimates that only one hundred who are both deaf and blind are appropriately placed, yet the country's total number of such children urgently requiring help is 1,600;

in New York State there are 500 deaf and/or otherwise handicapped for whom there are no places in special schools;

after the 1964 rubella epidemic (the United States's worst in a generation), 30,000 children were born handicapped, about 15,000 died before birth, and perhaps 5,000 who were born died in early infancy;

50 out of every 100 children born with rubella-induced birth defects have hearing problems, including 20 who will also develop brain damage or behavioral disturbances;

a scourge? a scourge, yes, and meningitis is another, though neither of these hit you;

then I see a report from Hong Kong that more than 100 deaf and dumb people in Liaoning province were recently cured by "a Liberation Army health team" and can now say "Long live chairman Mao" and sing "the East is Red" (no, they don't mean *you*);

one sixteen-year-old English boy, although totally deaf, won a major prize at the Derby College of Further Education presented by the Central Electricity Board to outstanding students, and no one will hire him, even though he only wants to be a tool setter;

but fifteen deaf mutes have joined the Lockheed-Georgia company, after six weeks' intensive training, to wire "squawk boxes" and other kinds of advanced electronic equipment for jet aircraft;

says Michel Eyquem, Seigneur de Montaigne (whom you can later on call Montee if you want): "Our deaf mutes dispute, argue, and tell stories by means of signs. . . . I have seen some so skillful and practical in that language that in truth they did not fall short of perfection in making themselves understood";

at the Eugene O'Neill Foundation, where forty deaf people study drama for three crammed weeks, everyone uses sign language, and well enough to permit exacting discussions of such things as philosophy, Greek drama, and the psychology of acting technique;

a report to the Federal Government stated that teachers in the United Kingdom "cannot understand their own pupils";

children who learn one mode of signing in school evolve another clandestine one for use outside;

signing, writes one deaf clergyman (who "has depended on signing for most of his lifetime"), "is the natural language of those who lack the gift of lip-reading, and it can be grammatical to a degree";

Sir Richard Paget, originator of the Paget sign system, concluded that the mouth gestures of speech were first derived from hand gestures, which means that sign language was the original form of all speech;

and revisions of his system—based not on finger spelling but on one sign for each word—remind me of Chinese and Arabic inasmuch as words with a common theme (time, birds, fire, etc.) have their own basic sign;

and that is good to know, because the signs relate to words and not merely to events, and the closer the relationship the more chance *you* have to having both, of becoming a genuine oral-aural-optical-manual-mental deaf eclectic, capable of appreciating in more ways than one the National Theater of the Deaf signing ensemble the poem of E. E. Cummings called "I will wade out," and then you too will find your thighs steeped in burning flowers, swallow the sun into your mouth, and leap into the air's ripeness. Verbally, that is. And, once you have enough words (by whatever means), you'll be able to do the impossible in yet another way (other than painting, than dreaming): talk to axolotls, to ask them how they got the way they are; send radio messages to both the Concorde jet prototypes wherever they are; describe the biggest slide in all the world. . . .

I've just discovered *The Sanders Reader*, the longhand book which Alexander Graham Bell composed for a six-year-old deaf boy called George Sanders; it employs not only heavier writing to show vocal emphasis, but also a visible speech code, developed by Bell's father, which indicates the position and action of throat, tongue, and lips—and it, the latter, looks like music (or four Mandys, drawn by you, on the first horizontal slide):

⌠(▭ʔʔʔʔ).

And the thickness and thinness of the strokes, for loud and soft, for emphasis and the lessening of it, take us back to Chinese and Japanese, with which you and I have not yet done.

All of us have so far only scratched the surface of the things that can be done for you: there's loads to try. Synesthesia comes after (forgive it! forgive it!) *sign*-esthesia. What of *Robinson Crusoe* done over into ITA?

You're willing? Crusoe-Kreutznaer and all?

I'll do it.

Ie'll dω it.

Why then Ile fit you.

Hieronimo's mad againe.

And when we were deaf, staying in the bundocks,
My eagle, she took me up on her slide,
And I was unwilling. She said, *Ee, Ee,*
Hold on tight. And down I sped.
On the slides, you really feel free.

I write, much of the time, am paid to talk in the winter.

And, unlike you, I never knew how it feels to learn my tenses through colors (though, I must confess, I was always drawn to Rimbaud's *Sonnet des voyelles* and its doctrine of the color of sounds:

A black, E white, I red, O blue, U green . . .

Et cetera (what color is that? what color is the future? what color is the first day of the rest of your life?).

Let's relax.

Your small being is no longer in the old turmoil.

Your small being is now rather big.

Your teacher *drew* a green slide but *wrote* "red tree" under it, just to see what you would do. You leapt to your feet and raved at the error; then, saying it, tried to write "gεεd slied," which you say as *geed zlide*.

An epiphany. Wonderful.

And now, to keep the record straight, let's add your colors, which you know and love: *boo, geed, re', wy.*

Ellow we've already had.

But not yet *black,* I think, although you've now got *der-ee* (dirty, which black is) and *dowl* (towel), which you like to blacken anyway.

Off we go again, my voracity more anxious (I hope) than my anxiety's voracious. I hope that's what I meant; I *hope* that's the better of the two ill things; there's almost just too much. . . . There's sometimes too much too soon, but there's also too little and too late: I remember vividly a photograph of a bright-eyed resident of a home for deaf women who had three or four dolls alongside her; "the little mother of dolls," the caption said;

I've read that regional accents are often more obvious to people who lip-read than to people who hear;

I've read an excerpt from an essay by a deaf boy who had been on a visit to the Netherlands and I like his prose style:

> When we got off the ship it was so hot and the Dutch men gave us drinks. In the evening some of us went on a river bus. We saw the smallest house in the world. We went to Alkmaar to the cheese market. We saw a huge mechanical organ. Then we looked at the Dutch men carrying the sledge full of red ball cheese. Behind us there was a man making clogs. I bought a pair of red clogs. . . .

I've read about Montessori schools, the Model High School for the Deaf, and the discoveries of Bruno Bettelheim; but the piece of reading I most remember is an essay by a German whose special interest is dysmelia children: deaf children without arms, and his point was that deaf children with additional handicaps learn not for themselves or for school, but—and this more than any other children—for their parents. It's true of you: home is school as well as school is, and the aim of both places is to demand the maximum of you, to convert the world around you into your own private hothouse. Hence, at home, all the applause you receive for saying something such as "thumb" and the far from rigid wooing we subject you to. School, of course, isn't as much home as home is, but you *are* at home there (where you can have a birthday party and be clapped for being "gωd" and have a card from your teacher that says "wiτh luv"). School's a bit domestic, then, and home is school with a bit more histrionic pageantry and a lewder, more ingratiating mode of propaganda.

It's all a matter, I suppose, of our being flexible enough to encourage you into an educational opportunism, by which I mean an opportunism *non scholae sed vitae* (as the Latin proverb has it)—not for school but for life. And that entails forgetting the far end of decorum best exemplified by some lines in a film I saw the other day in which a British consular official and his small son got off a train somewhere in Spain and were met by some flunkey or other, who then said to the boy, "Pleased to meet you, Master [Whateverhisnamewas]." Moments later, father takes son aside in the full brunt of that Spanish sun and rebukes him: "We don't say 'Pleased to meet you.' " Not the done thing, not the elite formula.

Well, I hereby grant you *carte blanche* to add PTMY to your magnificent arsenal of solecisms and exempt you forthwith (as if you cared) from behavior requiring any degree of dehydrated stateliness. It can be a little nerve-racking to live with and go out with someone whose sense of "proper" behavior is as scant as yours is, but better that—better anything worse—than pernickety demands that would silence or annul you. "We are often," one seventeen-year-old deaf girl writes, "given withering looks when we try to make conversation, designed to make us feel embarrassed, and shut us up; they well serve their purpose. Such an attitude does not go a long way towards giving ourselves confidence—it has exactly the opposite effect, and it can be disheartening."

Add to that an observation of your mother's. Out in town with you (and invariably with a handicapped friend of yours along as well) she knows what sorts of looks you will all get, and before the looks even come. Staggered by your birdcall or by the abandon of your movements (you dance wherever you feel like dancing), the *hoi polloi* actually lose a second or two while standing to stare and then pout their troughing slots to hold back the offensive word which cannot come anyway, for no word is appropriately offensive enough for what they are thinking. Their eyes they tighten up as if to eliminate you from sight altogether, but not before they have flashed the glance that masks *There but for the grace of God go I* with *So that's the sort of woman who produces that sort of child.*

How to discomfit them is this: before they look away, your mother in a loud voice says something such as, *Come this way now, Auntie is taking you to . . .*, and at once the affronted faces of the true believers in well-behaved eugenics relax, granting instant exculpation and conferring a bonus to that selfless, altruistic woman for being a credit to society—society that doesn't care enough about these wretched children, and it's so nice to see the trusties having an afternoon out in the presence of a well-dressed, nicely spoken Norm instead of slung almost umbilically from the hand of the shameless dam who, one can be sure, had this visited upon her as a well-deserved punishment for some unmentionable, lubricious trespass.

What people cannot stand to think is that a child such as you was born in the ordinary way and not dumped on the doorstep by some night-traveling devil or mailed to the mother in installments, sender's name not given, as an incubus kit. Or bought cheap at Woolworth's, cut-rate at Macy's, given away as a free gift with any purchase of two hot-water bottles. It's justice, really, gone sour right before your eyes: these folk can't bear to think that it happens to the innocent (such as themselves), so they dream up sins for your sponsors to have committed. In other words, they don't like a universe that's absurd, a universe they can't understand; they can't bear the evidence of a quite impersonal, inexplicable organic mishap. But in their mock-retributive panic they manage to differentiate a little, so that blindness is sort of clean, with straight deafness not far behind—physical, almost, like *mutilés de guerre* and the club foot or even the hare lip—but *mental* handicap, for which there's no readily available automatic response, because after all it's something wrong in the chair in which the soul itself sits: *that* won't *do*.

After all (so the thinking runs if thinking it is), those who've got a clean hurt don't presume, don't get in the way; they gratefully accept such forbearing compassion as they can detect around them, looking up like sheep to be fed with pity, listening hard to the shuffles as good folk get out of the way of the skeletal tapping stick. It's beside the point that most people bellow at the deaf as if all the deaf are blockheads and don't even present their mouths to be read whether they bellow or not, or that most blind people will tell you they themselves get bellowed at as if they too are deaf and, also, get manhandled at pedestrian crossings by zealous would-be pilots.

All that is more or less clean stuff. What isn't is the way someone like you just assumes you are an exceptionally privileged person, free to sing out in ecstasy or pique, free to dance the dance of rage or untrammeled joy, free to touch someone and laugh or leer just because you find them hot or cold to the touch, spongy or furniture-hard. Or, when something tastes so finger-licking good, to get intimate with it and eat it with hands even though, usually, your table manners are mutinously suave. Usually you get about as good a reception as a mongol does and sometimes you get a better one because you don't look different and are in fact a girl of pretty generally acknowledged offbeat beauty. So you fool them by the score and then, just when they've eased back into the clammy upholstery of their preconceptions—another nicely mannered little girl!—you show your true colors and they at once build retrospective accusation into a swindled-looking indignation; why, they might even have patted your head and so exposed themselves to heaven knows what.

It may sound odd, but I think most people would prefer—if they have to see you at all as you taxi round (not that I mean *in* taxis so much) the streets and stores to renew your cosmetic supplies and add to your jet fleet and your museum load of umbrellas—if you had a big label against your chest like the publicly hanged, or if we had you on a leash attached to a pretty collar around your neck (pink for a girl), or if we upped your handicap and crammed you into a wheelchair with handcuffs and some form of a bridle, with maybe a bit for you to chomp on and as a crown the EEG electrodes which you think are hairdressing devices.

It would all be in the interests of the civilized part of the population who have to be protected at all costs and who, rather ineffectually, defend themselves with such weapon words as oddball, crank, nut, idiot, imbecile, moron. . . . Yet, to take only one example, a spastic is born every eight hours, against which fact I'll set the recently made assertion that less than a quarter of the population of New York City is mentally balanced. Statistics I don't need, but I know that for bringing out the latent handicaps in the adult who prides himself on being a regular guy, an *honnête homme,* a decent chap, there's nothing like a few handicapped children daring to pretend to equal rights. Because she knows this, the face of the handicapped child's mother develops a highly specialized expression compact of sangfroid and offensive-defensive readiness, for she has seen them all already and she knows that, when it comes to the crunch, most people only too gladly fall away (even the parent at times is tempted to).

Life, as an old professor of philosophy I knew once said, is an unloving crock of shit, as well as being all its wonderful selves as well. When I last saw him, a few months before he died, he told me he'd been staring at the sun and I asked had it recognized him and that, somehow, made the shit a little less unloving for him for a moment or two; or so he said. Let's end this vein by saying that the professionals in handicaps don't always tell the parents as much as they should and could, such is the wariness of the expert researcher; and this may well account for a lot of do-it-yourself antics such as we've practiced and proved with you, for a lot of the shopping-around for advice and diagnosis-upon-diagnosis that sometimes drives frustrated parents to fly with their child from London to Philadelphia and *vice versa,* from Washington to Toronto and *vice versa,* and also for the woeful gap there often is (although not in your case) between schools for the handicapped and ordinary schools and therefore, by extension, between the handicapped of all ages and the non-handicapped, so-called, of all ages.

Nature abhors a vacuum, as Spinoza said; but, I'll add, vacuums don't much trouble society, for it is in vacuums that the handicapped are most often found; where, having nothing to breathe, they make faces and no progress. There's often a vacuum too between the austere professional and the harassed parent; some consultants prefer amenable children to deal with and thus would prefer the mutest and the meekest of the deaf (which you are far from being), and others having got what information they need from a specific case (i.e., child), either lose their notes altogether (as in your case) or fail to transmit information to whatever school the child ends up in. "Seen but not heard" isn't quite the right phrase; most people would prefer handicapped children neither seen nor heard, so it is very bad when experts fail to make contact with them as individual people. On the one hand there are the scientific reasons for your being the way you are, which may or may not be discoverable; on the other hand, and even in the absence of scientific explanations, there has to be the art of bringing you up. In Warsaw these days, in the night, loutish types accost the nocturnal stroller with a brick which he either agrees to buy there and then or receives in the head. It's similar with handicapped children: one does what the situation enforces. Who knows? The brick may turn out to be gold and may especially delight, having been received in the dark.

I don't know if you've heard of *The Cosmic Sword* or *The Intoxicated Imperial Mistress,* or of Madame Sueschien Chang or Madame Yen-Wei Kwoh, but these are Chinese operas and Chinese opera singers that depend very largely on what Mei Lang-fang (the Chinese diva of our century) calls "highly concentrated expressions, or artistic exaggerations from daily life." The operas are Pekingese and the ladies are from Hong Kong, but the important fact is that the performances at the Commonwealth Institute in London are for the Commonwealth Society for the Deaf, which one newspaper calls "a rather tactless choice of charity." I can't for the life of me see why, it's not as if the deaf were obliged to go along to be frustrated; it's not as if they were being spared a dime in the street instead of having the receipts fed into the financial arteries of a multitude of component organizations. In fact I don't think the blind, children or adult, would mind an exhibition of paintings being staged on their behalf, or paraplegics mind receiving the proceeds from a charity soccer game played by the able-bodied. I respect the sensitivity that would take the part of deaf people against all possible forms of tactlessness, but I don't think the ladies from Hong Kong (who sing for charities only) are being tactless at all. There is little enough enlightened sympathy with the handicapped and I'm delighted to salute it when it occurs, but compassion can sometimes waste itself in overprotectiveness in matters that are picayune. The difference that really counts is between a performance which deaf people, if they attended it, might not perfectly hear but which helps them indirectly and, say, a discourteous bellow in a public place, which helps no one at all.

What I began to stay, though, was that you yourself might enjoy just contemplating those "highly concentrated expressions" and "artistic exaggerations," just as you enjoy the cardboard gargoyles hanging on our line in the living room and the color photographs of the latest Frankenstein monster (or "the Being" as he is sometimes gently called). And from what I know of handicapped children, were any one of the more fearsome monsters to promenade through your school at closing time, you and the rest of the children would follow him like the Pied Piper. One extreme receives another.

Speaking of operas and of not hearing them, I find myself irritated by the highbrow silence-cult of the last five years or so. "Silence" is one of the In words, you see, and language is such a trial, such a worthless sham, such an expense of the brahmin spirit in a waste of shame. Camus's "cry of the mind exhausted by its own rebellion" is followed by millions upon millions of words in which writers beat an ironical retreat from the word itself—the word that abstracts, that falsifies, that dehumanizes, that substitutes Apollo for Dionysus, that offers only the illusion of control and discipline, that launches ambition without nourishing the heart, that is clearly inferior to chemical equations and symbolic logic for the chore of describing what we know, that is so arbitrary a form of non-communication it is best employed—if at all—to expose its own fraudulence or in accidental, random works for which the "author" is not responsible at all. Anybody who's done any amount of so-called serious writing knows about all that and has surely, in his time, longed to succumb into pure alliteration with Joyce, into connotational percussion with Dylan Thomas, into the Cut Up Method of Brion Gysin with William Burroughs, into alphabet pictures with the concrete poets, into the All with Rimbaud, into Zero with Mallarmé. . . .

The only sincerity is in silence, the only ecstasy is that which remains unstated. Yet if we were to force all our exponents of anti-word into the near-worldlessness of someone such as you—make them live your life while remembering all the words they once had like toys of which they've been deprived—would they not run for the dictionary hills, heedless of the ironic subtlety of their former position and aching to devour the first bit of print they happened on and to talk with the first person they met? If not, you are surely in a most enviable condition that is likely to become the new vogue. Half the fun of pretending to repudiate words is being able to use words about doing it, but when you never had the words anyway you don't have the option and you don't have half the fun. It's one thing to say on papper that you hate words; it's quite another to be *you*, say, stranded in the middle of a city on your own, verbally knowing neither address nor street nor time nor currency nor native tongue.

Clearly enough, insofar as words concern me myself—setting these down hopefully for you, certainly for me, probably for others—it's an incontestable help to be able to address you, and very different from the long silences of our horse-play or our sittings-together in repose. You, in turn, in order to come closer to the medium in which I'm expressing myself, will soon be having modified hearing aids which will bring the sound in your ears almost up to what we would find the decibel equivalent of a jet aircraft, with engines on full, close at hand. So that, one day, I might be able to read Aesop's Fables to you or an abridged and simplified *Treasure Island;* hardly, I think, for many and many years, this prose, these words. Samuel Beckett, who agonizes about words more than anybody and uses them better than almost everybody, struck home to himself with one furtive-sounding axiom in *How It Is:* "Words have their utility the mud is mute."

And that juxtaposition, meaningful because we are none of us mud, is truly how it is. Not only do I want you to be the supreme Romantic who, in the words of Mario Praz, "listens to the prodigious concerts of his soul without attempting to translate them into notes"; I want you also to be able to go and buy a pound of butter. You live in a long emergency that is none of your own making; an emergency that has taught me two things: how precious any kind of language is, whether your eventual limit happens to be Edgar Rice Burroughs or Wittgenstein; and, under the stimulus of your unorthodox avidity, how hidebound the modern imagination is, how tame, how timid, how prosaic, when all the time it should be playing religiously in its own right, not only poking into physics and chemistry and natural history, but responding to the terror of non-being by creating what was not there before; which, essentially, is what it is for.

> Dear Dad.
>
> Thank you Mandy

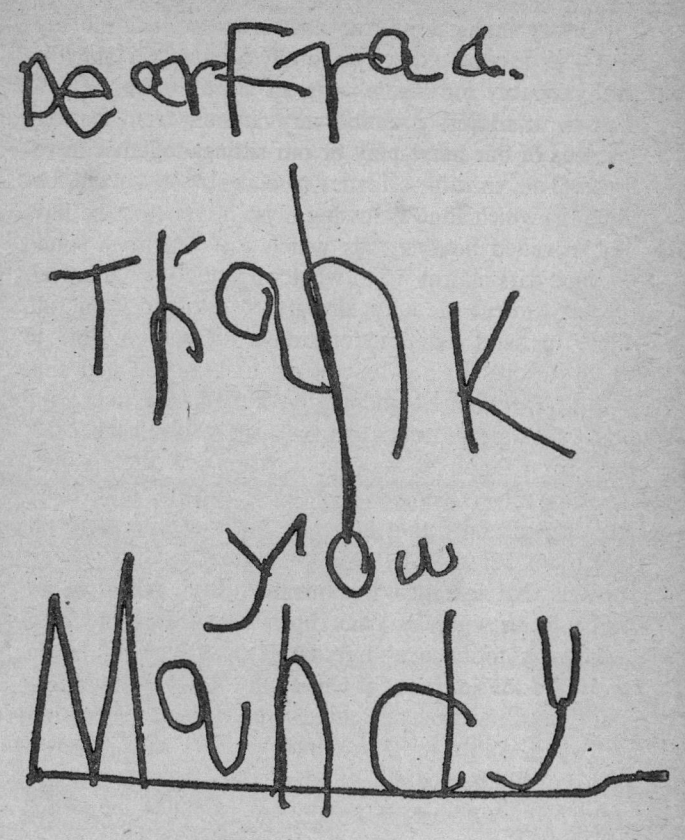

"Words have their utility..."
(*You thank my editor at Harper & Row for some Christmas tights.*)

It is like the day, some two years ago, when you were out playing in the frosted-over mud of the garden in a blue anorak with the hood laced firm under your chin, and pounding away at a tree with a small shovel; the phrase *royal-blue forester* flashed into my head and didn't go away again; something new, like the pantomime within these pages.

Christmas has come and all but gone, but you, who seize upon many things just as they are about to disappear, have held on to it in the form of a ritualized once-every-half-hour ecstasy you bring about by calling *Oo! Ba! Mandy!* and cupping one hand over your eyes. Then you sit as if carved in alabaster, or cuttlefish bone, while one of us goes out of the room to rewrap one of your many presents and ostentatiously smuggle it in again. Unable to contain yourself any longer, you pounce upon the bearer and rend the fancy paper, usually giving the contents the merest inspectional glance.

It isn't, for once, innocent greed; it's a mystery that you want repeated over and over again: the trim pageantry of wrappings, the flimsy strait-jacket of Scotch tape and silver string, the pretense and the tantalizing and the certainty that a parcel never lets you down. *Oo!* is for beauty, as *Ba!* is for present, and as we are for fetching and carrying—to and from the upstairs cache—toys whose existence you know of, but whose frequent vanishings and reappearances you complicitously accept. Even out of Christmas, that reliable messmass, you construct an event even more reliable that enables you to celebrate reliability every day. What is good you want to spread out and what is spread out you want to multiply, perhaps, until it becomes the whole world. The honey from the comb becomes your finger paint and your presents become presents of the mind.

Not that, for a second, you would let us secrete from you (even only to give back to you rewrapped) your Meccano erector set with electric motor. No, like a tin-and-cardboard Parthenon, this stays put, stacked on the roof of your doll's house—or, rather, the boxes do, emptied after we've built a windmill or a roundabout, or full after we've dismantled. Just now, though, nearly all the parts are locked together to form a two-foot-long hypodermic complete with six rotating needles driven by the tiny yellow motor. The vibration is enough to send the nuts spinning off the bolts, but you don't heed a flaw so trivial.

Zhok, you say, pointing at whoever is to play doc. Then: *nee'ul.*

And then you, or we, receive the rotating six-pronged injection from the spinning blunt needles, and you quiver, whichever role you are playing, with giddy giggles.

Mandy *zhok!*

Nee'ul. Then you scream the word.

Do you want to knit, like that, right in the middle of something else?

No, you don't. *Nee'ul* is also gun, so we find your cap-firing six-gun and you smile, a little scared because you know you will now have to fire it. But, with a face that tells us it isn't losing face at all, you set it down and leap across the room to your easel and begin to chalk or paint (depending on which side of it you're at) a huge Mandy or May, and tell us your name, which you have now exoticized into Mandy (or May) Weiss. Sometimes, though, it comes out as May Wet, which can be read as a water warning but which might simply mean you have it in mind to go up and see somebody sometime, or have someone come up to see you.

And therefore *must* you go around with your skirt or nightdress rolled up like a seaweed cummerbund high above your navel? And inch, hunch, your way backward through doors, tapping on the woodwork like an overgrown crab, and sometimes ending up further back than when you began, all this with your eyes almost shut and, across your face, a grin of silent refined irresponsibility directed at no one at all? You have cut the hair off all your Christmas dolls; there are five bristled skulls on the ledge above the bath, just as if a nit doctor had gone berserk after years of picking and scratching and just mowed the crop off all the heads in sight.

A'poo, you say. We don't know what this means; it isn't apple.

You follow it with *ba*, which we know.

Nee'ul?

No-o-o-o, you histrionically tell us. *Ba.*

Ba Beard?

You smile agreement, but we try, *try*, you further to see what you'll say.

Horse?

Hawz, no-o-o. *Ba. Oo, ba, Mandy. Out,* with one hand covering your eyes and with the other pointing at the ceiling. So we do it and then do it again, to make you use words.

You have become undiffident.

You overpower the mustered manpower of all of us.

One of the butterflies in the school play (a performance we looked forward to with intense misgiving), you broke out of your tall shuffle and skimmed off the stage to inspect the audience. At the school party your head teacher, somehow anticipating one of your flashpoint sorties, held you in comradely manner by the hand while the conjuror performed, but, needing to blow his nose, let you loose for a second or two, and there you were on the stage, wreck-helping with the act. I must say, though, you paid your debt in full: having quit the stage, you just as abruptly went back to it. All in your own time.

Your second school report shows what you have done with a year: you have usefully exhausted it. You appear, it says, to enjoy using your hearing aids and you vocalize spontaneously and continually. Wherever you go, you carry a small mirror in which to watch your mouth. You *lip-read* simple nouns, "aided by hearing." You imitate rhythm and intonation well; you repeat simple nouns; your vocabulary is increasing, although you do not often spontaneously talk. You *copy* simple nouns but indulge in no spontaneous written expression. Pre-reading you excel at: you match word to word and word to picture; but with numbers you are less ready, eagerly taking part in all practical activities but reluctant to count. Your drawing and painting are lively and original and at handwork you have good manual control. You demonstrate great interest in all creative activities and, I read, you embark on "self-initiated free play in the swimming pool with increasing confidence." And you are more willing to accept new classroom routines, less timid of large groups of children. Your hearing is still "difficult to assess," but, all in all, you have been cooperating very well, and "progress is evident." If that doesn't deserve a few words from me, I don't know what does.

Thinking of the LEM which you ingenuously watched assume position on the moon, I fancied you a lemming, the only one of your kind—self-led and self-pursued—half expecting any day your computer to give us an 1107 alarm threatening complete destruction of your erasable memory, or a 1201 that tells us you've no more storage space and no longer can accept inputs every two seconds; but I ban that fancy straight away. One day soon, perhaps, after you've had your hair washed and dried and are sitting in a soft, groomed peace with your head wrapped in the peasant-style scarf which makes you look somehow Russian and makes me call you Natasha Ilyanova Grushinskaya (a loved child has many names), you'll say something for which I'll reward you with a tube of space toothpaste that has adhesive cloth manufactured into it to prevent it from coming apart in the air: not *yummay,* which is the pacifier you've self-satirizingly begun asking for again, long after I thought you'd forgotten both the word and the thing; and not *gni,* the knitting you do with elfin, contrapuntal abandon; and not *bu'fly,* of which you were a cinnabar-colored specimen; but your old *yee* extended into what I think it has been all along. I mean *yes,* and so will you, even if—a prisoner at play in a garden enclosed with chicken wire, either running toward us with the fresh air coming off you like perfume or standing at your slide vibrant with ownership—you're still as incoherent as daily light, as vulnerable as uranium 235, and have an atom where an atom shouldn't be.